MznLnx

Missing Links Exam Preps

Exam Prep for

Financial Accounting

Harrison & Horngren, 7th Edition

The MznLnx Exam Prep is your link from the texbook and lecture to your exams.
The MznLnx Exam Preps are unauthorized and comprehensive reviews of your textbooks.

MznLnx

Rico
Publications

Exam Prep for Financial Accounting
7th Edition
Harrison & Horngren

Publisher: Raymond Houge
Assistant Editor: Michael Rouger
Text and Cover Designer: Lisa Buckner
Marketing Manager: Sara Swagger
Project Manager, Editorial Production: Jerry Emerson
Art Director: Vernon Lowerui

Product Manager: Dave Mason
Editorial Assitant: Rachel Guzmanji
Pedagogy: Debra Long
Cover Image: Jim Reed/Getty Images
Text and Cover Printer: City Printing, Inc.
Compositor: Media Mix, Inc.

Printed in the United States
ISBN:

For more information about our products, contact us at:
Dave.Mason@RicoPublications.com

For permission to use material from this text or product, submit a request online to:
Dave.Mason@RicoPublications.com

Contents

TO THE STUDENT

COMPREHENSIVE

The *MznLnx* Exam Prep series is designed to help you pass your exams. Editors at MznLnx review your textbooks and then prepare these practice exams to help you master the textbook material. Unlike study guides, workbooks, and practice tests provided by the texbook publisher and textbook authors, *MznLnx* gives you ***all*** of the material in each chapter in exam form, not just samples, so you can be sure to nail your exam.

MECHANICAL

The MznLnx Exam Prep series creates exams that will help you learn the subject matter as well as test you on your understanding. Each question is designed to help you master the concept. Just working through the exams, you gain an understanding of the subject--its a simple mechanical process that produces success.

INTEGRATED STUDY GUIDE AND REVIEW

MznLnx is not just a set of exams designed to test you, its also a comprehensive review of the subject content. Each exam question is also a review of the concept, making sure that you will get the answer correct without having to go to other sources of material. You learn as you go! Its the easiest way to pass an exam.

HUMOR

Studying can be tedious and dry. MznLnx's instructional design includes moderate humor within the exam questions on occassion, to break the tedium and revitalize the brain

1. In economics, _________ or _________ goods or real _________ refers to factors of production used to create goods or services that are not themselves significantly consumed (though they may depreciate) in the production process. _________ goods may be acquired with money or financial _________. In finance and accounting, _________ generally refers to financial wealth, especially that used to start or maintain a business.

a. Vyborg Appeal
b. Disclosure
c. Capital
d. Screening

2. _________ is a type of lease - the other being an operating lease. A _________ effectively allows a firm to finance the purchase of an asset, even if, strictly speaking, the firm never acquires the asset. Typically, a _________ will give the lessee control over an asset for a large proportion of the asset's useful life, providing them the benefits and risks of ownership.

a. Profitability index
b. Debt ratio
c. 3M Company
d. Finance lease

3. In accounting, _________ are considered liabilities of the business that are to be settled in cash within the fiscal year or the operating cycle, whichever period is longer.

For example accounts payable for goods, services or supplies that were purchased for use in the operation of the business and payable within a normal period of time would be _________.

Bonds, mortgages and loans that are payable over a term exceeding one year would be fixed liabilities.

a. Payroll
b. Treasury stock
c. Closing entries
d. Current liabilities

4. A _________ is a contract conferring a right on one person to possess property belonging to another person (called a landlord or lessor) to the exclusion of the owner landlord. It is a rental agreement between landlord and tenant. The relationship between the tenant and the landlord is called a tenancy, and the right to possession by the tenant is sometimes called a leasehold interest.

a. Robinson-Patman Act
b. Federal Sentencing Guidelines
c. Model Code of Professional Responsibility
d. Lease

5. In economic models, the _________ time frame assumes no fixed factors of production. Firms can enter or leave the marketplace, and the cost (and availability) of land, labor, raw materials, and capital goods can be assumed to vary. In contrast, in the short-run time frame, certain factors are assumed to be fixed, because there is not sufficient time for them to change.

a. Long-run
b. 3M Company
c. BMC Software, Inc.
d. Short-run

6. A _________, also referred to as a note payable in accounting, is a contract where one party (the maker or issuer) makes an unconditional promise in writing to pay a sum of money to the other (the payee), either at a fixed or determinable future time or on demand of the payee, under specific terms. They differ from IOUs in that they contain a specific promise to pay, rather than simply acknowledging that a debt exists.

The terms of a note typically include the principal amount, the interest rate if any, and the maturity date.

a. BMC Software, Inc.
b. 3M Company
c. BNSF Railway
d. Promissory note

7. In economics, the concept of the _________ refers to the decision-making time frame of a firm in which at least one factor of production is fixed. Costs which are fixed in the _________ have no impact on a firms decisions. For example a firm can raise output by increasing the amount of labour through overtime.

a. Long-run
b. 3M Company
c. BMC Software, Inc.
d. Short-run

8. _________ is that which is owed; usually referencing assets owed, but the term can also cover moral obligations and other interactions not requiring money. In the case of assets, _________ is a means of using future purchasing power in the present before a summation has been earned. Some companies and corporations use _________ as a part of their overall corporate finance strategy.

a. Loan
b. Debenture
c. Debt
d. Lender

9. In financial accounting, a _________ is defined as an obligation of an entity arising from past transactions or events, the settlement of which may result in the transfer or use of assets, provision of services or other yielding of economic benefits in the future.

a. Liability
b. Corporate governance
c. Vested
d. False Claims Act

10. _________ are formal records of a business' financial activities.

In British English, including United Kingdom company law, _________ are often referred to as accounts, although the term _________ is also used, particularly by accountants.

_________ provide an overview of a business' financial condition in both short and long term.

a. Statement of retained earnings
b. Notes to the financial statements
c. 3M Company
d. Financial statements

11. A _________ is a type of business entity in which partners (owners) share with each other the profits or losses of the business undertaking in which all have invested. _________s are often favored over corporations for taxation purposes, as the _________ structure does not generally incur a tax on profits before it is distributed to the partners (i.e. there is no dividend tax levied.) However, depending on the _________ structure and the jurisdiction in which it operates, owners of a _________ may be exposed to greater personal liability than they would as shareholders of a corporation.

a. Corporate governance
b. Resource Conservation and Recovery Act
c. National Information Infrastructure Protection Act
d. Partnership

12. In physics, and more specifically kinematics, _________ is the change in velocity over time. Because velocity is a vector, it can change in two ways: a change in magnitude and/or a change in direction. In one dimension, _________ is the rate at which something speeds up or slows down.

a. ABC Television Network
b. AIG
c. AMEX
d. Acceleration

13. _________ refers to any one of several methods by which a company, for 'financial accounting' and/or tax purposes, depreciates a fixed asset in such a way that the amount of depreciation taken each year is higher during the earlier years of an assete;s life. For financial accounting purposes, _________ is generally used when an asset is expected to be much more productive during its early years, so that depreciation expense will more accurately represent how much of an assete;s usefulness is being used up each year. For tax purposes, _________ provides a way of deferring corporate income taxes by reducing taxable income in current years, in exchange for increased taxable income in future years.

a. Accelerated depreciation
b. User charge
c. Indirect tax
d. Effective marginal tax rates

14. An _________ is a period with reference to which United Kingdom corporation tax is charged. It helps dictate when tax is paid on income and gains. An _________ begins whenever a company comes within the corporation tax charge, and whenever an _________ ends without the company ceasing to be within the charge.

a. AIG
b. ABC Television Network
c. AMEX
d. Accounting period

15. In accounting, _________ or carrying value is the value of an asset according to its balance sheet account balance. For assets, the value is based on the original cost of the asset less any depreciation, amortization or impairment costs made against the asset. Traditionally, a company's _________ is its total assets minus intangible assets and liabilities.

a. Generally accepted accounting principles
b. Matching principle
c. Depreciation
d. Book value

16. _________ is a term used in accounting, economics and finance to spread the cost of an asset over the span of several years.

In simple words we can say that _________ is the reduction in the value of an asset due to usage, passage of time, wear and tear, technological outdating or obsolescence, depletion, inadequacy, rot, rust, decay or other such factors.

In accounting, _________ is a term used to describe any method of attributing the historical or purchase cost of an asset across its useful life, roughly corresponding to normal wear and tear.

a. General ledger
b. Net profit
c. Current asset
d. Depreciation

17. _________ is a specific term used in companies' financial reporting from the company-whole point of view. Because that use excludes the effects of changing ownership interest, an economic measure of _________ is necessary for financial analysis from the shareholders' point of view

_________ is defined by the Financial Accounting Standards Board, or FASB, as 'the change in equity [net assets] of a business enterprise during a period from transactions and other events and circumstances from nonowner sources. It includes all changes in equity during a period except those resulting from investments by owners and distributions to owners.'

_________ is the sum of net income and other items that must bypass the income statement because they have not been realized, including items like an unrealized holding gain or loss from available for sale securities and foreign currency translation gains or losses.

a. Comprehensive income
b. 3M Company
c. BNSF Railway
d. BMC Software, Inc.

18. _________ is equal to the income that a firm has after subtracting costs and expenses from the total revenue. _________ can be distributed among holders of common stock as a dividend or held by the firm as retained earnings.

The items deducted will typically include tax expense, financing expense (interest expense), and minority interest. Likewise, preferred stock dividends will be subtracted too, though they are not an expense.

a. Long-term liabilities
b. Matching principle
c. Net income
d. Generally accepted accounting principles

19. In accounting, _________ has a very specific meaning. It is an outflow of cash or other valuable assets from a person or company to another person or company. This outflow of cash is generally one side of a trade for products or services that have equal or better current or future value to the buyer than to the seller.

a. AIG
b. ABC Television Network
c. AMEX
d. Expense

20. In business and finance accounting, _________ is equal to the gross profit minus overheads minus interest payable plus/minus one off items for a given time period (usually: accounting period.)

A common synonym for '_________' when discussing financial statements (which include a balance sheet and an income statement) is the bottom line. This term results from the traditional appearance of an income statement which shows all allocated revenues and expenses over a specified time period with the resulting summation on the bottom line of the report.

a. Salvage value
b. Net profit
c. Cost of goods sold
d. Treasury stock

21. _________ is the recording of the value of assets, liabilities, income, and expenses in the daybooks, journals, and ledgers, in which debit and credit entries are chronologically posted to record changes in value. _________ is often mistaken for accounting, which is the system of recording, verifying, and reporting such information. Practitioners of accounting are called accountants.

a. Bookkeeping
b. Double-entry bookkeeping
c. Debit and credit
d. Controlling account

22. A _________ is a party (e.g. person, organization, company, or government) that has a claim to the services of a second party. It is a person or institution to whom money is owed. The first party, in general, has provided some property or service to the second party under the assumption (usually enforced by contract) that the second party will return an equivalent property or service.

a. Par value
b. Payback period
c. Treasury company
d. Creditor

23. _________ is concerned with the provisions and use of accounting information to managers within organizations, to provide them with the basis to make informed business decisions that will allow them to be better equipped in their management and control functions.

In contrast to financial accountancy information, _________ information is:

- usually confidential and used by management, instead of publicly reported;
- forward-looking, instead of historical;
- pragmatically computed using extensive management information systems and internal controls, instead of complying with accounting standards.

This is because of the different emphasis: _________ information is used within an organization, typically for decision-making.

a. Nonassurance services
b. Governmental accounting
c. Grenzplankostenrechnung
d. Management accounting

24. An _________ is a term used in behavioral economics to describe those types of behaviors that impose costs on a person in the long-run that are not taken into account when making decisions in the present. Classical Economics discourages government from creating legislation that targets internalities, because it is assumed that the consumer takes these personal costs into account when paying for the good that causes the _________. For example, cigarettes should be taxed because of the negative consumption externalities that they impose, such as second-hand smoke, not because the smoker harms him or herself by smoking.

a. Authorised capital
b. Operating budget
c. Inventory turnover ratio
d. Internality

25. An _________ is a practitioner of accountancy, which is the measurement, disclosure or provision of assurance about financial information that helps managers, investors, tax authorities and other decision makers make resource allocation decisions.

The word '_________' is derived from the French 'Compter' which took its origin from the Latin 'Computare'. The word was formerly written in English as 'Accomptant', but in process of time the word, which was always pronounced by dropping the 'p', became gradually changed both in pronunciation and in orthography to its present form.

a. ABC Television Network
b. Accountant
c. AMEX
d. AIG

26. The _________ is the national, professional association of CPAs in the United States, with more than 330,000 members, including CPAs in business and industry, public practice, government, and education; student affiliates; and international associates. It sets ethical standards for the profession and U.S. auditing standards for audits of private companies; federal, state and local governments; and non-profit organizations.

Approximately 40% of its members are engaged in the practice of public accounting, in areas such as auditing, accounting, taxation, general business consulting, business valuation, personal financial planning and business technology.

a. AIG
b. ABC Television Network
c. Other postemployment benefits
d. American Institute of Certified Public Accountants

27. The general definition of an _________ is an evaluation of a person, organization, system, process, project or product. _________s are performed to ascertain the validity and reliability of information; also to provide an assessment of a system's internal control. The goal of an _________ is to express an opinion on the person/organization/system (etc) in question, under evaluation based on work done on a test basis.

a. Institute of Chartered Accountants of India
b. Audit regime
c. Assurance service
d. Audit

28. _________ is the statutory title of qualified accountants in the United States who have passed the Uniform _________ Examination and have met additional state education and experience requirements for certification as a _________. Individuals who have passed the Exam but have not either accomplished the required on-the-job experience or have previously met it but in the meantime have lapsed their continuing professional education are, in many states, permitted the designation '_________ Inactive' or an equivalent phrase. In most U.S. states, only _________s who are licensed are able to provide to the public attestation (including auditing) opinions on financial statements.

a. Certified Public Accountant
b. Chartered Certified Accountant
c. Certified General Accountant
d. Chartered Accountant

29. A _________ is a non-profit organization seeking to further a particular profession, the interests of individuals engaged in that profession, and the public interest.

The roles of these _________s have been variously defined: 'A group of people in a learned occupation who are entrusted with maintaining control or oversight of the legitimate practice of the occupation;' also a body acting 'to safeguard the public interest;' organizations which 'represent the interest of the professional practitioners,' and so 'act to maintain their own privileged and powerful position as a controlling body.'

Such bodies generally strive to achieve a balance between these two often conflicting mandates. Though professional bodies often act to protect the public by maintaining and enforcing standards of training and ethics in their profession, they often also act like a cartel or a labor union for the members of the profession, though this description is commonly rejected by the body concerned.

a. HFMA
b. Freddie Mac
c. MicroStrategy
d. Professional association

30. _________ of something is, in finance, the adding together of interest or different investments over a period of time such as atoms (1 - the act or process of accruing; 2 - the amount that accrues.) It holds specific meanings in accounting and payroll.

_________, in accounting, describes the accounting method known as _________ basis, whereby revenues and expenses are recognized when they are accrued, i.e. accumulated (earned or incurred), regardless when the actual cash is received or paid out.

a. Earnings before interest, taxes, depreciation and amortization
b. Accounts receivable
c. Assets
d. Accrual

31. _________ is a method of accounting whereby economic activities (rather than cash flow) of financial events are considered, because of two complementary principles, which (together) determine the point, at which expenses and revenues are recognized. According to revenue recognition principle, revenues are realized when earned, whether or not they are received in cash.
a. Accrual basis accounting
b. Accrual
c. Accrued revenue
d. Earnings before interest, taxes, depreciation and amortization

32. In accounting and organizational theory, _________ is defined as a process effected by an organization's structure, work and authority flows, people and management information systems, designed to help the organization accomplish specific goals or objectives. It is a means by which an organization's resources are directed, monitored, and measured. It plays an important role in preventing and detecting fraud and protecting the organization's resources, both physical (e.g., machinery and property) and intangible (e.g., reputation or intellectual property such as trademarks.)
a. Internal control
b. Auditor independence
c. Audit committee
d. Audit risk

33. The term _________ usually refers to a company that is permitted to offer its registered securities (stock, bonds, etc.) for sale to the general public, typically through a stock exchange, or occasionally a company whose stock is traded over the counter (OTC) via market makers who use non-exchange quotation services.

The term '_________' may also refer to a company owned by the government.

a. Professional association
b. Governmental Accounting Standards Board
c. Public company
d. MicroStrategy

34. A sole _________, or simply _________ is a type of business entity which legally has no separate existence from its owner. Hence, the limitations of liability enjoyed by a corporation and limited liability partnerships do not apply to sole proprietors. All debts of the business are debts of the owner.
a. Safety stock
b. Pre-determined overhead rate
c. Free cash flow
d. Proprietorship

35. In business and accounting, _________ are everything of value that is owned by a person or company. It is a claim on the property your income of a borrower. The balance sheet of a firm records the monetary value of the _________ owned by the firm.
a. Accounts receivable
b. Assets
c. Accrual basis accounting
d. Earnings before interest, taxes, depreciation and amortization

36. _________ is the process of matching and comparing figures from accounting records against those presented on a bank statement. Less any items which have no relation to the bank statement, the balance of the accounting ledger should reconcile (match) to the balance of the bank statement.

_________ allows companies or individuals to compare their account records to the bank's records of their account balance in order to uncover any possible discrepancies.

a. Bank reconciliation
b. Lower of Cost or Market
c. Credit memo
d. Bankruptcy prediction

37. A _________ is a body of elected or appointed members who jointly oversee the activities of a company or organization. The body sometimes has a different name, such as board of trustees, board of governors, board of managers, or executive board. It is often simply referred to as 'the board.'

A board's activities are determined by the powers, duties, and responsibilities delegated to it or conferred on it by an authority outside itself.

a. Consumer protection laws
b. Board of directors
c. Hospital Survey and Construction Act
d. Chief Financial Officers Act of 1990

38. A _________ or chief executive is one of the highest-ranking corporate officer (executive) or administrator in charge of total management. An individual selected as President and _________ of a corporation, company, organization, or agency, reports to the board of directors. In internal communication and press releases, many companies capitalize the term and those of other high positions, even when they are not proper nouns.

a. Chief executive officer
b. Return on equity
c. Return on assets
d. Kohlberg Kravis Roberts ' Co

39. _________ are payments made by a corporation to its shareholder members. It is the portion of corporate profits paid out to stockholders. When a corporation earns a profit or surplus, that money can be put to two uses: it can either be re-invested in the business (called retained earnings), or it can be paid to the shareholders as a dividend.

a. Dividend stripping
b. Dividend yield
c. Dividend payout ratio
d. Dividends

40. The _________ is a private, not-for-profit organization whose primary purpose is to develop generally accepted accounting principles (GAAP) within the United States in the public's interest. The Securities and Exchange Commission (SEC) designated the _________ as the organization responsible for setting accounting standards for public companies in the U.S. It was created in 1973, replacing the Accounting Principles Board and the Committee on Accounting Procedure of the American Institute of Certified Public Accountants. The _________'s mission is 'to establish and improve standards of financial accounting and reporting for the guidance and education of the public, including issuers, auditors, and users of financial information.'

The _________ is not a governmental body.

a. Governmental Accounting Standards Board
b. Public company
c. Fannie Mae
d. Financial Accounting Standards Board

41. _________ is the term used to refer to the standard framework of guidelines for financial accounting used in any given jurisdiction. _________ includes the standards, conventions, and rules accountants follow in recording and summarizing transactions, and in the preparation of financial statements.

Financial accounting information must be assembled and reported objectively.

a. Long-term liabilities
b. General ledger
c. Generally accepted accounting principles
d. Current asset

42. A mutual shareholder or _________ is an individual or company (including a corporation) that legally owns one or more shares of stock in a joint stock company. A company's shareholders collectively own that company. Thus, the typical goal of such companies is to enhance shareholder value.

a. Growth investing
b. Stock split
c. 3M Company
d. Stockholder

43. In an economy, production, consumption and exchange are carried out by two basic _________: the firm and the household.

a. AIG
b. AMEX
c. Economic units
d. ABC Television Network

44. _________ was a maxim coined by Josiah Warren, indicating a (prescriptive) version of the labor theory of value. Warren maintained that the just compensation for labor (or for its product) could only be an equivalent amount of labor (or a product embodying an equivalent amount.) Thus, profit, rent, and interest were considered unjust economic arrangements.

a. Politicized issue
b. BMC Software, Inc.
c. 3M Company
d. Cost the limit of price

45. _________, also called fair price (in a commonplace conflation of the two distinct concepts), is a concept used in finance and economics, defined as a rational and unbiased estimate of the potential market price of a good, service, or asset, taking into account such objective factors as:

- acquisition/production/distribution costs, replacement costs, or costs of close substitutes
- actual utility at a given level of development of social productive capability
- supply vs. demand

and subjective factors such as

- risk characteristics
- cost of capital
- individually perceived utility

In accounting, _________ is used as an estimate of the market value of an asset (or liability) for which a market price cannot be determined (usually because there is no established market for the asset.) Under GAAP (FAS 157), _________ is the amount at which the asset could be bought or sold in a current transaction between willing parties, or transferred to an equivalent party, other than in a liquidation sale. This is used for assets whose carrying value is based on mark-to-market valuations; for assets carried at historical cost, the _________ of the asset is not used. One example of where _________ is an issue is a College kitchen with a cost of $2 million which was built 5 years ago.

a. Fair value
b. BNSF Railway
c. BMC Software, Inc.
d. 3M Company

46. In economics, _________ is a rise in the general level of prices of goods and services in an economy over a period of time. When the general price level rises, each unit of currency buys fewer goods and services; consequently, _________ is also a decline in the real value of money--a loss of purchasing power in the medium of exchange which is also the monetary unit of account in the economy. A chief measure of general price-level _________ is the general _________ rate, which is the percentage change in a general price index (normally the Consumer Price Index) over time.

a. Opportunity cost
b. Inflation
c. AIG
d. ABC Television Network

47. In economics, business, retail, and accounting, a _________ is the value of money that has been used up to produce something, and hence is not available for use anymore. In economics, a _________ is an alternative that is given up as a result of a decision. In business, the _________ may be one of acquisition, in which case the amount of money expended to acquire it is counted as _________.

a. Cost of quality
b. Prime cost
c. Cost
d. Cost allocation

48. _________ refers to a business or organization attempting to acquire goods or services to accomplish the goals of the enterprise. Though there are several organizations that attempt to set standards in the _________ process, processes can vary greatly between organizations. Typically the word e;_________e; is not used interchangeably with the word e;procuremente;, since procurement typically includes Expediting, Supplier Quality, and Traffic and Logistics (T'L) in addition to _________.

a. Free port
b. Consignor
c. Supply chain
d. Purchasing

49. The basic _________ is the foundation for the double-entry bookkeeping system. It shows how assets were financed: either by borrowing money from someone (liability) or by paying your own money (shareholders' equity.)

Assets = Liabilities + (Shareholders or Owners equity)

For example: A student buys a computer for $945.

a. AIG
b. Accounting equation
c. ABC Television Network
d. AMEX

50. _________ are liabilities with a future benefit over one year, such as notes payable that mature greater than one year.

In accounting, the _________ are shown on the right wing of the balance-sheet representing the sources of funds, which are generally bounded in form of capital assets.

Examples of _________ are debentures, mortgage loans and other bank loans (note: not all bank loans are long term as not all are paid over a period greater than a year, the example is bridging loan.)

a. Cash basis accounting
b. Book value
c. Long-term liabilities
d. Gross sales

51. In accounting/accountancy, _________ are journal entries usually made at the end of an accounting period to allocate income and expenditure to the period in which they actually occurred. The revenue recognition principle is the basis of making _________ that pertain to unearned and accrued revenues under accrual-basis accounting. They are sometimes called Balance Day adjustments because they are made on balance day.

a. Accrual
b. Earnings before interest, taxes, depreciation and amortization
c. Adjusting entries
d. Accrued expense

52. In financial accounting, a _________ or statement of financial position is a summary of a person's or organization's balances. Assets, liabilities and ownership equity are listed as of a specific date, such as the end of its financial year. A _________ is often described as a snapshot of a company's financial condition.

a. Financial statements
b. Statement of retained earnings
c. 3M Company
d. Balance sheet

53. _________ is a file or account that contains money that a person or company owes to suppliers, but has not paid yet (a form of debt.) When you receive an invoice you add it to the file, and then you remove it when you pay. Thus, the A/P is a form of credit that suppliers offer to their purchasers by allowing them to pay for a product or service after it has already been received.

a. Accrual
b. Accounts receivable
c. Accounts payable
d. Earnings before interest, taxes, depreciation and amortization

54. In finance, a _________ is a debt security, in which the authorized issuer owes the holders a debt and, depending on the terms of the _________, is obliged to pay interest (the coupon) and/or to repay the principal at a later date, termed maturity. It is a formal contract to repay borrowed money with interest at fixed intervals.

Thus a _________ is like a loan: the issuer is the borrower, the _________ holder is the lender, and the coupon is the interest.

a. Bond
b. Coupon rate
c. Revenue bonds
d. Zero-coupon bond

55. _________ is a form of corporation equity ownership represented in the securities. It is a stock whose dividends are based on market fluctuations. It is dangerous in comparison to preferred shares and some other investment options, in that in the event of bankruptcy, _________ investors receive their funds after preferred stock holders, bondholders, creditors, etc. On the other hand, common shares on average perform better than preferred shares or bonds over time.

a. 3M Company
b. Common stock
c. Growth investing
d. Stock split

56. _________, also known as property, plant, and equipment (PP&E), is a term used in accountancy for assets and property which cannot easily be converted into cash. This can be compared with current assets such as cash or bank accounts, which are described as liquid assets. In most cases, only tangible assets are referred to as fixed.

a. Minority interest
b. Fixed asset
c. Subledger
d. Bankruptcy prediction

57. _________ is the state or fact of exclusive rights and control over property, which may be an object, land/real estate or intellectual property. An _________ right is also referred to as title.

_________ is the key building block in the development of the capitalist socio-economic system.

a. ABC Television Network
b. Administrative proceeding
c. Ownership
d. Encumbrance

58. _________ is any physical or virtual entity that is owned by an individual or jointly by a group of individuals. An owner of _________ has the right to consume, sell, rent, mortgage, transfer and exchange his or her _________. Important widely-recognized types of _________ include real _________, personal _________ (other physical possessions), and intellectual _________ (rights over artistic creations, inventions, etc.), although the latter is not always as widely recognized or enforced.

a. Disclosure requirement
b. Fiduciary
c. Property
d. Primary authority

59. In finance, a _________ is a type of bond that can be converted into shares of stock in the issuing company, usually at some pre-announced ratio. It is a hybrid security with debt- and equity-like features. Although it typically has a low coupon rate, the holder is compensated with the ability to convert the bond to common stock, usually at a substantial discount to the stock's market value.

a. Coupon rate
b. Zero-coupon bond
c. Zero-coupon
d. Convertible bond

60. A _________, also client, buyer or purchaser is the buyer or user of the paid products of an individual or organization, mostly called the supplier or seller. This is typically through purchasing or renting goods or services.

a. 3M Company
b. BNSF Railway
c. Customer
d. BMC Software, Inc.

61. In economics a _________ is an entity that owes a debt to someone else. The entity may be an individual, a firm, a government, a company or other legal person. The counterparty is called a creditor.

a. Shares authorized
b. Debtor
c. Fair market value
d. Segregated portfolio company

62. _________ is a fee paid on borrowed assets. It is the price paid for the use of borrowed money , or, money earned by deposited funds .Assets that are sometimes lent with _________ include money, shares, consumer goods through hire purchase, major assets such as aircraft, and even entire factories in finance lease arrangements. The _________ is calculated upon the value of the assets in the same manner as upon money.

a. Insolvency
b. AIG
c. ABC Television Network
d. Interest

63. _________ are sometimes the same as net worth, or shareholders' equity - assets minus liabilities. The term _________ is commonly used with charities or not for profit entities. Although these entities don't make money, it is important to maintain reasonable reserves to help future growth.

a. Net interest spread
b. Net assets
c. Sortino ratio
d. Debtor days

64. A _________ is the transfer of wealth from one party (such as a person or company) to another. A _________ is usually made in exchange for the provision of goods, services or both, or to fulfill a legal obligation.

The simplest and oldest form of _________ is barter, the exchange of one good or service for another.

a. BMC Software, Inc.
b. Payment
c. Payee
d. 3M Company

65. In accounting, a _________ is an asset on the balance sheet which is expected to be sold or otherwise used up in the near future, usually within one year, or one business cycle - whichever is longer. Typical _________s include cash, cash equivalents, accounts receivable, inventory, the portion of prepaid accounts which will be used within a year, and short-term investments.

On the balance sheet, assets will typically be classified into _________s and long-term assets.

a. Deferred
b. Pro forma
c. General ledger
d. Current asset

66. _________ is a company's financial statement that indicates how the revenue is transformed into the net income The purpose of the _________ is to show managers and investors whether the company made or lost money during the period being reported.

The important thing to remember about an _________ is that it represents a period of time.

a. AMEX
b. AIG
c. ABC Television Network
d. Income statement

67. In financial accounting, _________ or cost of sales includes the direct costs attributable to the production of the goods sold by a company. This amount includes the materials cost used in creating the goods along with the direct labor costs used to produce the good. It excludes indirect expenses such as distribution costs and sales force costs.

a. Reorder point
b. FIFO and LIFO accounting
c. Cost of goods sold
d. 3M Company

68. In bookkeeping, accounting, and finance, _________ are operating revenues earned by a company when it sells its products. Revenue (_________) are reported directly on the income statement as Sales or _________.

In financial ratios that use income statement sales values, 'sales' refers to _________, not gross sales.

a. Deferred
b. Matching principle
c. Historical cost
d. Net sales

69. A _________ is the pinnacle activity involved in selling products or services in return for money or other compensation. It is an act of completion of a commercial activity.

A _________ is completed by the seller, the owner of the goods.

a. Maturity
b. Tertiary sector of economy
c. Sale
d. High yield stock

70. The _________ is one of the basic financial statements as per Generally Accepted Accounting Principles, and it explains the changes in a company's retained earnings over the reporting period. It breaks down changes affecting the account, such as profits or losses from operations, dividends paid, and any other items charged or credited to retained earnings. A retained earnings statement is required by Generally Accepted Accounting Principles whenever comparative balance sheets and income statements are presented.

a. Statement of retained earnings
b. Financial statements
c. 3M Company
d. Notes to the financial statements

71. _________ is the balance of the amounts of cash being received and paid by a business during a defined period of time, sometimes tied to a specific project. Measurement of _________ can be used

- to evaluate the state or performance of a business or project.
- to determine problems with liquidity. Being profitable does not necessarily mean being liquid. A company can fail because of a shortage of cash, even while profitable.
- to project rate of returns. The time of _________s into and out of projects are used as inputs to financial models such as internal rate of return, and net present value.
- to examine income or growth of a business when it is believed that accrual accounting concepts do not represent economic realities. Alternately, _________ can be used to 'validate' the net income generated by accrual accounting.

_________ as a generic term may be used differently depending on context, and certain _________ definitions may be adapted by analysts and users for their own uses. Common terms include operating _________ and free _________.

a. Controlling interest
b. Commercial paper
c. Flow-through entity
d. Cash flow

72. _________ is one of a series of accounting transactions dealing with the billing of customers who owe money to a person, company or organization for goods and services that have been provided to the customer. In most business entities this is typically done by generating an invoice and mailing or electronically delivering it to the customer, who in turn must pay it within an established timeframe called credit or payment terms.

An example of a common payment term is Net 30, meaning payment is due in the amount of the invoice 30 days from the date of invoice.

a. Adjusting entries
b. Accrued revenue
c. Accounts receivable
d. Accrual

73. _________ are securities that can be easily converted into cash. Such securities will generally have highly liquid markets allowing the security to be sold at a reasonable price very quickly.This is a usual feature in real estate .

a. Tracking stock
b. 3M Company
c. BMC Software, Inc.
d. Marketable

74. A _________ is a fungible, negotiable instrument representing financial value. they are broadly categorized into debt securities (such as banknotes, bonds and debentures), and equity securities; e.g., common stocks. The company or other entity issuing the _________ is called the issuer.

a. 3M Company
b. BMC Software, Inc.
c. Tracking stock
d. Security

75. An _________ is a tax levied on the financial income of people, corporations, or other legal entities. Various _________ systems exist, with varying degrees of tax incidence. Income taxation can be progressive, proportional, or regressive.

a. Ordinary income
b. Implied level of government service
c. Individual Retirement Arrangement
d. Income tax

76. _________, in law and economics, is a form of risk management primarily used to hedge against the risk of a contingent loss. _________ is defined as the equitable transfer of the risk of a loss, from one entity to another, in exchange for a premium, and can be thought of as a guaranteed small loss to prevent a large, possibly devastating loss. An insurer is a company selling the _________; an insured is the person or entity buying the _________.

a. Insurance
b. AMEX
c. ABC Television Network
d. AIG

77. _________ are defined as identifiable non-monetary assets that cannot be seen, touched or physically measured, which are created through time and/or effort and that are identifiable as a separate asset. There are two primary forms of intangibles - legal intangibles (such as trade secrets (e.g., customer lists), copyrights, patents, trademarks, and goodwill) and competitive intangibles (such as knowledge activities (know-how, knowledge), collaboration activities, leverage activities, and structural activities.) Legal intangibles are known under the generic term intellectual property and generate legal property rights defensible in a court of law.

a. Intangible assets
b. AIG
c. Overhead
d. ABC Television Network

78. _________ represents claims for which formal instruments of credit are issued as evidence of debt, such as a promissory note. The credit instrument normally requires the debtor to pay interest and extends for time periods of 60-90 days or longer.

a. Moving average
b. Restricted stock
c. Public offering
d. Notes receivable

79. _________ refers to services paid for in advance. Examples include tolls, pay as you go cell phones, and stored-value cards such as gift cards and preloaded credit cards. _________ accounts are assets, and they are increased by debiting the account(s.)

a. BMC Software, Inc.
b. BNSF Railway
c. 3M Company
d. Prepaid

80. _________, in accrual accounting, is any account where the asset or liability is not realized until a future date (accounting period), e.g. annuities, charges, taxes, income, etc. The _________ item may be carried, dependent on type of deferral, as either an asset or liability.

a. Payroll
b. Cash basis accounting
c. Pro forma
d. Deferred

81. A _________ is a compensation, usually financial, received by a worker in exchange for their labor.

Compensation in terms of _________s is given to worker and compensation in terms of salary is given to employees. Compensation is a monetary benefits given to employees in returns of the services provided by them.

a. BMC Software, Inc.
b. Retirement plan
c. Wage
d. 3M Company

82. In financial accounting, a _________ or Statement of cash flows is a financial statement that shows a company's flow of cash. The money coming into the business is called cash inflow, and money going out from the business is called cash outflow. The statement shows how changes in balance sheet and income accounts affect cash and cash equivalents, and breaks the analysis down to operating, investing, and financing activities.

a. 3M Company
b. BMC Software, Inc.
c. Cash flow statement
d. BNSF Railway

83. A _________ is a set of exclusive rights granted by a state to an inventor or his assignee for a limited period of time in exchange for a disclosure of an invention.

The procedure for granting _________s, the requirements placed on the _________ee and the extent of the exclusive rights vary widely between countries according to national laws and international agreements. Typically, however, a _________ application must include one or more claims defining the invention which must be new, inventive, and useful or industrially applicable.

a. Trust indenture
b. Negligence
c. FLSA
d. Patent

84. _________ can be regarded as an outcome of mental processes (cognitive process) leading to the selection of a course of action among several alternatives. Every _________ process produces a final choice. The output can be an action or an opinion of choice.

a. BNSF Railway
b. Decision making
c. 3M Company
d. BMC Software, Inc.

85. _________ in a corporation means to have control of a large enough block of voting stock shares in a company such that no one stock holder or coalition of stock holders can successfully oppose a motion. In theory this normally means that _________ would be 50% of the voting shares plus one.

In practice, though, _________ can be far less than that, as it is rare that 100% of a company's voting shareholders actively vote.

a. Controlling interest
b. Public offering
c. Preferred stock
d. Participating preferred stock

86. A _________ is a company that owns enough voting stock in another firm to control management and operations by influencing or electing its board of directors; the second company being deemed as a subsidiary of the _________. The definition of a _________ differs from jurisdiction to jurisdiction, with the definition normally being defined by way of laws dealing with companies in that jurisdiction.

The _________-subsidiary company relationship is defined by Part 1.2, Division 6, Section 46 of the Corporations Act 2001 (Cth), which states:

A body corporate (in this section called the first body) is a subsidiary of another body corporate if, and only if:

(a) the other body:

(i) controls the composition of the first body's board; or

(ii) is in a position to cast, or control the casting of, more than one-half of the maximum number of votes that might be cast at a general meeting of the first body; or

(iii) holds more than one-half of the issued share capital of the first body (excluding any part of that issued share capital that carries no right to participate beyond a specified amount in a distribution of either profits or capital); or

(b) the first body is a subsidiary of a subsidiary of the other body.

a. 3M Company
b. Subsidiary
c. BMC Software, Inc.
d. Parent company

87. A _________, in business matters, is an entity that is controlled by a bigger and more powerful entity. The controlled entity is called a company, corporation, or limited liability company, and the controlling entity is called its parent (or the parent company.) The reason for this distinction is that a lone company cannot be a _________ of any organization; only an entity representing a legal fiction as a separate entity can be a _________.

a. Subsidiary
b. Parent company
c. BMC Software, Inc.
d. 3M Company

1. The basic _________ is the foundation for the double-entry bookkeeping system. It shows how assets were financed: either by borrowing money from someone (liability) or by paying your own money (shareholders' equity.)

Assets = Liabilities + (Shareholders or Owners equity)

For example: A student buys a computer for $945.

a. AMEX
b. ABC Television Network
c. Accounting equation
d. AIG

2. _________ is one of a series of accounting transactions dealing with the billing of customers who owe money to a person, company or organization for goods and services that have been provided to the customer. In most business entities this is typically done by generating an invoice and mailing or electronically delivering it to the customer, who in turn must pay it within an established timeframe called credit or payment terms.

An example of a common payment term is Net 30, meaning payment is due in the amount of the invoice 30 days from the date of invoice.

a. Accrued revenue
b. Accounts receivable
c. Accrual
d. Adjusting entries

3. In business and accounting, _________ are everything of value that is owned by a person or company. It is a claim on the property your income of a borrower. The balance sheet of a firm records the monetary value of the _________ owned by the firm.

a. Accounts receivable
b. Accrual basis accounting
c. Earnings before interest, taxes, depreciation and amortization
d. Assets

4. In economics, _________ or _________ goods or real _________ refers to factors of production used to create goods or services that are not themselves significantly consumed (though they may depreciate) in the production process. _________ goods may be acquired with money or financial _________. In finance and accounting, _________ generally refers to financial wealth, especially that used to start or maintain a business.

a. Capital
b. Vyborg Appeal
c. Screening
d. Disclosure

5. In accounting, _________ has a very specific meaning. It is an outflow of cash or other valuable assets from a person or company to another person or company. This outflow of cash is generally one side of a trade for products or services that have equal or better current or future value to the buyer than to the seller.

a. ABC Television Network
b. AMEX
c. AIG
d. Expense

6. _________, in law and economics, is a form of risk management primarily used to hedge against the risk of a contingent loss. _________ is defined as the equitable transfer of the risk of a loss, from one entity to another, in exchange for a premium, and can be thought of as a guaranteed small loss to prevent a large, possibly devastating loss. An insurer is a company selling the _________; an insured is the person or entity buying the _________.

a. Insurance
b. ABC Television Network
c. AMEX
d. AIG

7. In financial accounting, a _________ is defined as an obligation of an entity arising from past transactions or events, the settlement of which may result in the transfer or use of assets, provision of services or other yielding of economic benefits in the future.

a. Corporate governance
b. False Claims Act
c. Liability
d. Vested

8. _________ refers to services paid for in advance. Examples include tolls, pay as you go cell phones, and stored-value cards such as gift cards and preloaded credit cards. _________ accounts are assets, and they are increased by debiting the account(s.)

a. BMC Software, Inc.
b. 3M Company
c. BNSF Railway
d. Prepaid

9. _________, in accrual accounting, is any account where the asset or liability is not realized until a future date (accounting period), e.g. annuities, charges, taxes, income, etc. The _________ item may be carried, dependent on type of deferral, as either an asset or liability.

a. Pro forma
b. Payroll
c. Cash basis accounting
d. Deferred

10. In accounting/accountancy, _________ are journal entries usually made at the end of an accounting period to allocate income and expenditure to the period in which they actually occurred. The revenue recognition principle is the basis of making _________ that pertain to unearned and accrued revenues under accrual-basis accounting. They are sometimes called Balance Day adjustments because they are made on balance day.

a. Accrued expense
b. Accrual
c. Earnings before interest, taxes, depreciation and amortization
d. Adjusting entries

11. In economics, business, retail, and accounting, a _________ is the value of money that has been used up to produce something, and hence is not available for use anymore. In economics, a _________ is an alternative that is given up as a result of a decision. In business, the _________ may be one of acquisition, in which case the amount of money expended to acquire it is counted as _________.

a. Cost allocation
b. Cost of quality
c. Prime cost
d. Cost

12. A _________, also client, buyer or purchaser is the buyer or user of the paid products of an individual or organization, mostly called the supplier or seller. This is typically through purchasing or renting goods or services.

a. BNSF Railway
b. Customer
c. 3M Company
d. BMC Software, Inc.

13. _________ is a term used in accounting, economics and finance to spread the cost of an asset over the span of several years.

In simple words we can say that _________ is the reduction in the value of an asset due to usage, passage of time, wear and tear, technological outdating or obsolescence, depletion, inadequacy, rot, rust, decay or other such factors.

In accounting, _________ is a term used to describe any method of attributing the historical or purchase cost of an asset across its useful life, roughly corresponding to normal wear and tear.

a. Current asset
b. General ledger
c. Net profit
d. Depreciation

14. _________ is a specific term used in companies' financial reporting from the company-whole point of view. Because that use excludes the effects of changing ownership interest, an economic measure of _________ is necessary for financial analysis from the shareholders' point of view

_________ is defined by the Financial Accounting Standards Board, or FASB, as 'the change in equity [net assets] of a business enterprise during a period from transactions and other events and circumstances from nonowner sources. It includes all changes in equity during a period except those resulting from investments by owners and distributions to owners.'

_________ is the sum of net income and other items that must bypass the income statement because they have not been realized, including items like an unrealized holding gain or loss from available for sale securities and foreign currency translation gains or losses.

a. BMC Software, Inc.
b. Comprehensive income
c. BNSF Railway
d. 3M Company

15. _________ is a file or account that contains money that a person or company owes to suppliers, but has not paid yet (a form of debt.) When you receive an invoice you add it to the file, and then you remove it when you pay. Thus, the A/P is a form of credit that suppliers offer to their purchasers by allowing them to pay for a product or service after it has already been received.

a. Accounts receivable
b. Earnings before interest, taxes, depreciation and amortization
c. Accrual
d. Accounts payable

16. _________ are liabilities which have occurred, but have not been paid or logged under accounts payable during an accounting period; in other words, obligations for goods and services provided to a company for which invoices have not yet been received. Examples would include accrued wages payable, accrued sales tax payable, and accrued rent payable.

There are two general types of _________:

- Routine and recurring
- Infrequent or non-routine

Most companies pay their employees on a predetermined schedule. Let's say that the 'Imaginary company Ltd.' pays its employees each Friday for the hours worked that week.

a. AMEX
b. Accrued liabilities
c. ABC Television Network
d. AIG

17. In finance, a _________ is a debt security, in which the authorized issuer owes the holders a debt and, depending on the terms of the _________, is obliged to pay interest (the coupon) and/or to repay the principal at a later date, termed maturity. It is a formal contract to repay borrowed money with interest at fixed intervals.

Thus a _________ is like a loan: the issuer is the borrower, the _________ holder is the lender, and the coupon is the interest.

a. Coupon rate
b. Revenue bonds
c. Zero-coupon bond
d. Bond

18. _________ is a form of corporation equity ownership represented in the securities. It is a stock whose dividends are based on market fluctuations. It is dangerous in comparison to preferred shares and some other investment options, in that in the event of bankruptcy, _________ investors receive their funds after preferred stock holders, bondholders, creditors, etc. On the other hand, common shares on average perform better than preferred shares or bonds over time.

a. 3M Company
b. Common stock
c. Stock split
d. Growth investing

19. In accounting, _________ are considered liabilities of the business that are to be settled in cash within the fiscal year or the operating cycle, whichever period is longer.

For example accounts payable for goods, services or supplies that were purchased for use in the operation of the business and payable within a normal period of time would be _________.

Bonds, mortgages and loans that are payable over a term exceeding one year would be fixed liabilities.

a. Treasury stock
b. Closing entries
c. Payroll
d. Current liabilities

20. In economic models, the _________ time frame assumes no fixed factors of production. Firms can enter or leave the marketplace, and the cost (and availability) of land, labor, raw materials, and capital goods can be assumed to vary. In contrast, in the short-run time frame, certain factors are assumed to be fixed, because there is not sufficient time for them to change.

a. 3M Company
b. Long-run
c. BMC Software, Inc.
d. Short-run

21. _________ are liabilities with a future benefit over one year, such as notes payable that mature greater than one year.

In accounting, the _________ are shown on the right wing of the balance-sheet representing the sources of funds, which are generally bounded in form of capital assets.

Examples of _________ are debentures, mortgage loans and other bank loans (note: not all bank loans are long term as not all are paid over a period greater than a year, the example is bridging loan.)

a. Book value
b. Cash basis accounting
c. Gross sales
d. Long-term liabilities

22. A _________, also referred to as a note payable in accounting, is a contract where one party (the maker or issuer) makes an unconditional promise in writing to pay a sum of money to the other (the payee), either at a fixed or determinable future time or on demand of the payee, under specific terms. They differ from IOUs in that they contain a specific promise to pay, rather than simply acknowledging that a debt exists.

The terms of a note typically include the principal amount, the interest rate if any, and the maturity date.

a. BNSF Railway
b. BMC Software, Inc.
c. 3M Company
d. Promissory note

23. In finance, a _________ is a type of bond that can be converted into shares of stock in the issuing company, usually at some pre-announced ratio. It is a hybrid security with debt- and equity-like features. Although it typically has a low coupon rate, the holder is compensated with the ability to convert the bond to common stock, usually at a substantial discount to the stock's market value.

a. Zero-coupon bond
b. Convertible bond
c. Zero-coupon
d. Coupon rate

24. _________ is that which is owed; usually referencing assets owed, but the term can also cover moral obligations and other interactions not requiring money. In the case of assets, _________ is a means of using future purchasing power in the present before a summation has been earned. Some companies and corporations use _________ as a part of their overall corporate finance strategy.

a. Loan
b. Lender
c. Debenture
d. Debt

25. In economics a _________ is an entity that owes a debt to someone else. The entity may be an individual, a firm, a government, a company or other legal person. The counterparty is called a creditor.

a. Fair market value
b. Shares authorized
c. Debtor
d. Segregated portfolio company

26. _________ is a fee paid on borrowed assets. It is the price paid for the use of borrowed money , or, money earned by deposited funds .Assets that are sometimes lent with _________ include money, shares, consumer goods through hire purchase, major assets such as aircraft, and even entire factories in finance lease arrangements. The _________ is calculated upon the value of the assets in the same manner as upon money.

a. AIG
b. Interest
c. Insolvency
d. ABC Television Network

27. _________ is the state or fact of exclusive rights and control over property, which may be an object, land/real estate or intellectual property. An _________ right is also referred to as title.

_________ is the key building block in the development of the capitalist socio-economic system.

a. Administrative proceeding
b. Encumbrance
c. ABC Television Network
d. Ownership

28. A _________ is the transfer of wealth from one party (such as a person or company) to another. A _________ is usually made in exchange for the provision of goods, services or both, or to fulfill a legal obligation.

The simplest and oldest form of _________ is barter, the exchange of one good or service for another.

a. BMC Software, Inc.
b. 3M Company
c. Payee
d. Payment

29. _________ are payments made by a corporation to its shareholder members. It is the portion of corporate profits paid out to stockholders. When a corporation earns a profit or surplus, that money can be put to two uses: it can either be re-invested in the business (called retained earnings), or it can be paid to the shareholders as a dividend.

a. Dividend payout ratio
b. Dividend yield
c. Dividend stripping
d. Dividends

30. _________ are formal records of a business' financial activities.

In British English, including United Kingdom company law, _________ are often referred to as accounts, although the term _________ is also used, particularly by accountants.

_________ provide an overview of a business' financial condition in both short and long term.

a. Statement of retained earnings
b. 3M Company
c. Notes to the financial statements
d. Financial statements

31. An _________ is a period with reference to which United Kingdom corporation tax is charged. It helps dictate when tax is paid on income and gains. An _________ begins whenever a company comes within the corporation tax charge, and whenever an _________ ends without the company ceasing to be within the charge.

a. AIG
b. ABC Television Network
c. AMEX
d. Accounting period

32. A mutual shareholder or _________ is an individual or company (including a corporation) that legally owns one or more shares of stock in a joint stock company. A company's shareholders collectively own that company. Thus, the typical goal of such companies is to enhance shareholder value.

a. Growth investing
b. Stock split
c. Stockholder
d. 3M Company

33. In financial accounting, a _________ or statement of financial position is a summary of a person's or organization's balances. Assets, liabilities and ownership equity are listed as of a specific date, such as the end of its financial year. A _________ is often described as a snapshot of a company's financial condition.

a. 3M Company
b. Statement of retained earnings
c. Balance sheet
d. Financial statements

34. _________ is the balance of the amounts of cash being received and paid by a business during a defined period of time, sometimes tied to a specific project. Measurement of _________ can be used

- to evaluate the state or performance of a business or project.
- to determine problems with liquidity. Being profitable does not necessarily mean being liquid. A company can fail because of a shortage of cash, even while profitable.
- to project rate of returns. The time of _________s into and out of projects are used as inputs to financial models such as internal rate of return, and net present value.
- to examine income or growth of a business when it is believed that accrual accounting concepts do not represent economic realities. Alternately, _________ can be used to 'validate' the net income generated by accrual accounting.

_________ as a generic term may be used differently depending on context, and certain _________ definitions may be adapted by analysts and users for their own uses. Common terms include operating _________ and free _________.

a. Cash flow
b. Commercial paper
c. Flow-through entity
d. Controlling interest

35. _________ is a company's financial statement that indicates how the revenue is transformed into the net income The purpose of the _________ is to show managers and investors whether the company made or lost money during the period being reported.

The important thing to remember about an _________ is that it represents a period of time.

a. Income statement
b. AIG
c. ABC Television Network
d. AMEX

36. In financial accounting, a _________ or Statement of cash flows is a financial statement that shows a company's flow of cash. The money coming into the business is called cash inflow, and money going out from the business is called cash outflow. The statement shows how changes in balance sheet and income accounts affect cash and cash equivalents, and breaks the analysis down to operating, investing, and financing activities.

a. 3M Company
b. Cash flow statement
c. BNSF Railway
d. BMC Software, Inc.

37. The _________ is one of the basic financial statements as per Generally Accepted Accounting Principles, and it explains the changes in a company's retained earnings over the reporting period. It breaks down changes affecting the account, such as profits or losses from operations, dividends paid, and any other items charged or credited to retained earnings. A retained earnings statement is required by Generally Accepted Accounting Principles whenever comparative balance sheets and income statements are presented.

a. Notes to the financial statements
b. Financial statements
c. 3M Company
d. Statement of retained earnings

38. _________ is equal to the income that a firm has after subtracting costs and expenses from the total revenue. _________ can be distributed among holders of common stock as a dividend or held by the firm as retained earnings.

The items deducted will typically include tax expense, financing expense (interest expense), and minority interest. Likewise, preferred stock dividends will be subtracted too, though they are not an expense.

a. Net income
b. Generally accepted accounting principles
c. Matching principle
d. Long-term liabilities

39. _________ and credit are formal bookkeeping and accounting terms. They are the most fundamental concepts in accounting, representing the two records that one party in a transaction makes on its records, transferring a money balance from one account to another, one representing a reduction of liability or increase in asset, and the other representing a balancing increase in liability or reduction of asset.

Introduction

_________s and credits are a system of notation used in accounting to keep track of money movements (transactions) into and out of an account.

a. Debit and credit
b. Bookkeeping
c. Debit
d. Cookie jar accounting

40. _________ is a system of financial accounting where each transaction is recorded in at least two accounts: at least one account is debited and at least one account is credited, so that the total debits of the transaction equal to the total credits. For example, if Company A sells an item to Company B, and Company B pays by cheque, then the bookkeeper of Company A credits the account 'Sales' and debits the account 'Bank'. Conversely, the bookkeeper of Company B debits the account 'Purchases' and credits the account 'Bank'.

a. Double-entry bookkeeping
b. Bookkeeping
c. Debit and credit
d. Cookie jar accounting

41. The term _________, derived from the distinctive T shape, is frequently used when discussing or analyzing accounting or business transactions. _________s are used to represent general ledger accounts.

Typically one or more Ts are drawn on a white board or blank piece of paper. A general ledger account name or number is then written above each T. Debit entries are recorded on the left side of the 'T' and credit entries are recorded on the right side of the 'T'.

a. 3M Company
b. T account
c. BNSF Railway
d. BMC Software, Inc.

42. A _________ has several related meanings:

- a daily record of events or business; a private _________ is usually referred to as a diary.
- a newspaper or other periodical, in the literal sense of one published each day;
- many publications issued at stated intervals, such as magazines, or scholarly academic _________s, or the record of the transactions of a society, are often called _________s. Although _________ is sometimes used, erroneously, as a synonym for 'magazine,' in academic use, a _________ refers to a serious, scholarly publication, most often peer-reviewed. A non-scholarly magazine written for an educated audience about an industry or an area of professional activity is usually called a professional magazine.

The word 'journalist' for one whose business is writing for the public press has been in use since the end of the 17th century.

Open access _________s are scholarly _________s that are available to the reader without financial or other barrier other than access to the internet itself. Some are subsidized, and some require payment on behalf of the author. Subsidized _________s are financed by an academic institution or a government information center.

a. BMC Software, Inc.
b. BNSF Railway
c. 3M Company
d. Journal

43. A _________ is a contract conferring a right on one person to possess property belonging to another person (called a landlord or lessor) to the exclusion of the owner landlord. It is a rental agreement between landlord and tenant. The relationship between the tenant and the landlord is called a tenancy, and the right to possession by the tenant is sometimes called a leasehold interest.

a. Model Code of Professional Responsibility
b. Lease
c. Federal Sentencing Guidelines
d. Robinson-Patman Act

44. In accounting, the _________ is a worksheet listing the balance at a certain date, of each ledger account in two columns, namely debit and credit. Under the double-entry system, in any transaction the total of any debits must equal the total of any credits, so in a _________ the total of the debit side should always be equal to the total of the credit side. The _________ thus serves as a tool to detect errors, which can result in the totals not being equal.

a. Bottom line
b. Trial balance
c. Depreciation
d. Current asset

45. _________ is a list of the accounts including a unique number of each allowing to locate it in each ledger. The list is typically arranged in the order of the customary appearance of accounts in the financial statements. A _________ can track a specific financial information.

a. Journal entry
b. General ledger
c. Chart of accounts
d. General journal

46. _________ is the value on a given date of a future payment or series of future payments, discounted to reflect the time value of money and other factors such as investment risk. _________ calculations are widely used in business and economics to provide a means to compare cash flows at different times on a meaningful 'like to like' basis.

The most commonly applied model of the time value of money is compound interest.

a. Net present value
b. Future value
c. Present value
d. 3M Company

1. _________ of something is, in finance, the adding together of interest or different investments over a period of time such as atoms (1 - the act or process of accruing; 2 - the amount that accrues.) It holds specific meanings in accounting and payroll.

_________, in accounting, describes the accounting method known as _________ basis, whereby revenues and expenses are recognized when they are accrued, i.e. accumulated (earned or incurred), regardless when the actual cash is received or paid out.

a. Accounts receivable
b. Earnings before interest, taxes, depreciation and amortization
c. Assets
d. Accrual

2. _________ is a method of accounting whereby economic activities (rather than cash flow) of financial events are considered, because of two complementary principles, which (together) determine the point, at which expenses and revenues are recognized. According to revenue recognition principle, revenues are realized when earned, whether or not they are received in cash.

a. Accrual
b. Earnings before interest, taxes, depreciation and amortization
c. Accrued revenue
d. Accrual basis accounting

3. In financial accounting, a _________ or statement of financial position is a summary of a person's or organization's balances. Assets, liabilities and ownership equity are listed as of a specific date, such as the end of its financial year. A _________ is often described as a snapshot of a company's financial condition.

a. 3M Company
b. Statement of retained earnings
c. Financial statements
d. Balance sheet

4. _________ is a method of accounting whereby cash flow of financial events is considered. The method recognizes revenues when cash is received and recognizes expenses when cash is paid out. In cash accounting, revenues and expenses are also called cash receipts and cash payments respectively.

a. Treasury stock
b. Closing entries
c. Net sales
d. Cash basis accounting

5. The _________ is a private, not-for-profit organization whose primary purpose is to develop generally accepted accounting principles (GAAP) within the United States in the public's interest. The Securities and Exchange Commission (SEC) designated the _________ as the organization responsible for setting accounting standards for public companies in the U.S. It was created in 1973, replacing the Accounting Principles Board and the Committee on Accounting Procedure of the American Institute of Certified Public Accountants. The _________'s mission is 'to establish and improve standards of financial accounting and reporting for the guidance and education of the public, including issuers, auditors, and users of financial information.'

The _________ is not a governmental body.

a. Fannie Mae
b. Public company
c. Governmental Accounting Standards Board
d. Financial Accounting Standards Board

6. _________ is the term used to refer to the standard framework of guidelines for financial accounting used in any given jurisdiction. _________ includes the standards, conventions, and rules accountants follow in recording and summarizing transactions, and in the preparation of financial statements.

Financial accounting information must be assembled and reported objectively.

a. General ledger
b. Current asset
c. Long-term liabilities
d. Generally accepted accounting principles

7. _________ is a company's financial statement that indicates how the revenue is transformed into the net income The purpose of the _________ is to show managers and investors whether the company made or lost money during the period being reported.

The important thing to remember about an _________ is that it represents a period of time.

a. ABC Television Network
b. AMEX
c. AIG
d. Income statement

8. A _________ is the pinnacle activity involved in selling products or services in return for money or other compensation. It is an act of completion of a commercial activity.

A _________ is completed by the seller, the owner of the goods.

a. Sale
b. High yield stock
c. Tertiary sector of economy
d. Maturity

9. In business and accounting, _________ are everything of value that is owned by a person or company. It is a claim on the property your income of a borrower. The balance sheet of a firm records the monetary value of the _________ owned by the firm.

a. Accrual basis accounting
b. Accounts receivable
c. Earnings before interest, taxes, depreciation and amortization
d. Assets

10. _________ is the balance of the amounts of cash being received and paid by a business during a defined period of time, sometimes tied to a specific project. Measurement of _________ can be used

- to evaluate the state or performance of a business or project.
- to determine problems with liquidity. Being profitable does not necessarily mean being liquid. A company can fail because of a shortage of cash, even while profitable.
- to project rate of returns. The time of _________s into and out of projects are used as inputs to financial models such as internal rate of return, and net present value.
- to examine income or growth of a business when it is believed that accrual accounting concepts do not represent economic realities. Alternately, _________ can be used to 'validate' the net income generated by accrual accounting.

_________ as a generic term may be used differently depending on context, and certain _________ definitions may be adapted by analysts and users for their own uses. Common terms include operating _________ and free _________.

a. Controlling interest
b. Commercial paper
c. Flow-through entity
d. Cash flow

11. In accounting, _________ has a very specific meaning. It is an outflow of cash or other valuable assets from a person or company to another person or company. This outflow of cash is generally one side of a trade for products or services that have equal or better current or future value to the buyer than to the seller.

a. Expense
b. ABC Television Network
c. AMEX
d. AIG

12. In financial accounting, a _________ is defined as an obligation of an entity arising from past transactions or events, the settlement of which may result in the transfer or use of assets, provision of services or other yielding of economic benefits in the future.

a. Corporate governance
b. Vested
c. False Claims Act
d. Liability

13. _________ is equal to the income that a firm has after subtracting costs and expenses from the total revenue. _________ can be distributed among holders of common stock as a dividend or held by the firm as retained earnings.

The items deducted will typically include tax expense, financing expense (interest expense), and minority interest. Likewise, preferred stock dividends will be subtracted too, though they are not an expense.

a. Matching principle
b. Generally accepted accounting principles
c. Net income
d. Long-term liabilities

14. An _________ is a period with reference to which United Kingdom corporation tax is charged. It helps dictate when tax is paid on income and gains. An _________ begins whenever a company comes within the corporation tax charge, and whenever an _________ ends without the company ceasing to be within the charge.

a. AMEX
b. AIG
c. ABC Television Network
d. Accounting period

15. _________ are formal records of a business' financial activities.

In British English, including United Kingdom company law, _________ are often referred to as accounts, although the term _________ is also used, particularly by accountants.

_________ provide an overview of a business' financial condition in both short and long term.

a. Notes to the financial statements
b. Financial statements
c. Statement of retained earnings
d. 3M Company

16. In financial accounting, a _________ or Statement of cash flows is a financial statement that shows a company's flow of cash. The money coming into the business is called cash inflow, and money going out from the business is called cash outflow. The statement shows how changes in balance sheet and income accounts affect cash and cash equivalents, and breaks the analysis down to operating, investing, and financing activities.

a. BMC Software, Inc.
b. 3M Company
c. BNSF Railway
d. Cash flow statement

17. In physics, and more specifically kinematics, _________ is the change in velocity over time. Because velocity is a vector, it can change in two ways: a change in magnitude and/or a change in direction. In one dimension, _________ is the rate at which something speeds up or slows down.

a. AMEX
b. Acceleration
c. ABC Television Network
d. AIG

18. _________ refers to any one of several methods by which a company, for 'financial accounting' and/or tax purposes, depreciates a fixed asset in such a way that the amount of depreciation taken each year is higher during the earlier years of an assete;s life. For financial accounting purposes, _________ is generally used when an asset is expected to be much more productive during its early years, so that depreciation expense will more accurately represent how much of an assete;s usefulness is being used up each year. For tax purposes, _________ provides a way of deferring corporate income taxes by reducing taxable income in current years, in exchange for increased taxable income in future years.

a. Indirect tax
b. User charge
c. Effective marginal tax rates
d. Accelerated depreciation

19. An _________ is a practitioner of accountancy, which is the measurement, disclosure or provision of assurance about financial information that helps managers, investors, tax authorities and other decision makers make resource allocation decisions.

The word '_________' is derived from the French 'Compter' which took its origin from the Latin 'Computare'. The word was formerly written in English as 'Accomptant', but in process of time the word, which was always pronounced by dropping the 'p', became gradually changed both in pronunciation and in orthography to its present form.

a. AIG
b. ABC Television Network
c. Accountant
d. AMEX

20. A _________, also client, buyer or purchaser is the buyer or user of the paid products of an individual or organization, mostly called the supplier or seller. This is typically through purchasing or renting goods or services.

a. BMC Software, Inc.
b. 3M Company
c. BNSF Railway
d. Customer

21. _________ is a term used in accounting, economics and finance to spread the cost of an asset over the span of several years.

In simple words we can say that _________ is the reduction in the value of an asset due to usage, passage of time, wear and tear, technological outdating or obsolescence, depletion, inadequacy, rot, rust, decay or other such factors.

In accounting, _________ is a term used to describe any method of attributing the historical or purchase cost of an asset across its useful life, roughly corresponding to normal wear and tear.

a. Current asset
b. Depreciation
c. General ledger
d. Net profit

22. _________ is a specific term used in companies' financial reporting from the company-whole point of view. Because that use excludes the effects of changing ownership interest, an economic measure of _________ is necessary for financial analysis from the shareholders' point of view

_________ is defined by the Financial Accounting Standards Board, or FASB, as 'the change in equity [net assets] of a business enterprise during a period from transactions and other events and circumstances from nonowner sources. It includes all changes in equity during a period except those resulting from investments by owners and distributions to owners.'

_________ is the sum of net income and other items that must bypass the income statement because they have not been realized, including items like an unrealized holding gain or loss from available for sale securities and foreign currency translation gains or losses.

a. BMC Software, Inc.
b. BNSF Railway
c. 3M Company
d. Comprehensive income

23. A _________ is the transfer of wealth from one party (such as a person or company) to another. A _________ is usually made in exchange for the provision of goods, services or both, or to fulfill a legal obligation.

The simplest and oldest form of _________ is barter, the exchange of one good or service for another.

a. Payee
b. 3M Company
c. BMC Software, Inc.
d. Payment

24. _________ is a cornerstone of accrual accounting together with the revenue recognition principle. They both determine the accounting period, in which revenues and expenses are recognized. According to the principle, expenses are recognized when obligations are (1) incurred (usually when goods are transferred or services rendered, e.g. sold), and (2) offset against recognized revenues, which were generated from those expenses (related on the cause-and-effect basis), no matter when cash is paid out.

a. Payroll
b. Net sales
c. Matching principle
d. Current liabilities

25. In economics, business, retail, and accounting, a _________ is the value of money that has been used up to produce something, and hence is not available for use anymore. In economics, a _________ is an alternative that is given up as a result of a decision. In business, the _________ may be one of acquisition, in which case the amount of money expended to acquire it is counted as _________.

a. Cost of quality
b. Cost
c. Prime cost
d. Cost allocation

26. In accounting/accountancy, _________ are journal entries usually made at the end of an accounting period to allocate income and expenditure to the period in which they actually occurred. The revenue recognition principle is the basis of making _________ that pertain to unearned and accrued revenues under accrual-basis accounting. They are sometimes called Balance Day adjustments because they are made on balance day.

a. Earnings before interest, taxes, depreciation and amortization
b. Adjusting entries
c. Accrual
d. Accrued expense

27. In accounting, the _________ is a worksheet listing the balance at a certain date, of each ledger account in two columns, namely debit and credit. Under the double-entry system, in any transaction the total of any debits must equal the total of any credits, so in a _________ the total of the debit side should always be equal to the total of the credit side. The _________ thus serves as a tool to detect errors, which can result in the totals not being equal.

a. Current asset
b. Depreciation
c. Trial balance
d. Bottom line

28. _________, in law and economics, is a form of risk management primarily used to hedge against the risk of a contingent loss. _________ is defined as the equitable transfer of the risk of a loss, from one entity to another, in exchange for a premium, and can be thought of as a guaranteed small loss to prevent a large, possibly devastating loss. An insurer is a company selling the _________; an insured is the person or entity buying the _________.

a. ABC Television Network
b. AIG
c. AMEX
d. Insurance

29. _________ refers to services paid for in advance. Examples include tolls, pay as you go cell phones, and stored-value cards such as gift cards and preloaded credit cards. _________ accounts are assets, and they are increased by debiting the account(s.)

a. 3M Company
b. BMC Software, Inc.
c. BNSF Railway
d. Prepaid

30. _________, is a liability with an uncertain timing or amount, but where the uncertainty is not significant enough to qualify it as a provision. An example is an unpaid obligation to pay for goods or services received FROM a counterpart, while cash for them is to be paid out in a latter accounting period when its amount is deducted from _________s.

a. Accrual basis accounting
b. Assets
c. Accounts receivable
d. Accrued expense

31. _________ is an asset, such as unpaid proceeds from a delivery of goods or services, at which such income item is earned and the related revenue item is recognized, while cash for them is to be received in a latter period, when its amount is deducted from the _________.

a. Accrued expense
b. Accounts receivable
c. Accrued revenue
d. Assets

32. In accounting, _________ are considered liabilities of the business that are to be settled in cash within the fiscal year or the operating cycle, whichever period is longer.

For example accounts payable for goods, services or supplies that were purchased for use in the operation of the business and payable within a normal period of time would be _________.

Bonds, mortgages and loans that are payable over a term exceeding one year would be fixed liabilities.

a. Payroll
b. Closing entries
c. Current liabilities
d. Treasury stock

33. In economic models, the _________ time frame assumes no fixed factors of production. Firms can enter or leave the marketplace, and the cost (and availability) of land, labor, raw materials, and capital goods can be assumed to vary. In contrast, in the short-run time frame, certain factors are assumed to be fixed, because there is not sufficient time for them to change.

a. BMC Software, Inc.
b. Short-run
c. 3M Company
d. Long-run

34. _________ are liabilities with a future benefit over one year, such as notes payable that mature greater than one year.

In accounting, the _________ are shown on the right wing of the balance-sheet representing the sources of funds, which are generally bounded in form of capital assets.

Examples of _________ are debentures, mortgage loans and other bank loans (note: not all bank loans are long term as not all are paid over a period greater than a year, the example is bridging loan.)

a. Book value
b. Gross sales
c. Long-term liabilities
d. Cash basis accounting

35. _________, in accrual accounting, is any account where the asset or liability is not realized until a future date (accounting period), e.g. annuities, charges, taxes, income, etc. The _________ item may be carried, dependent on type of deferral, as either an asset or liability.

a. Cash basis accounting
b. Deferred
c. Pro forma
d. Payroll

36. _________ is any physical or virtual entity that is owned by an individual or jointly by a group of individuals. An owner of _________ has the right to consume, sell, rent, mortgage, transfer and exchange his or her _________. Important widely-recognized types of _________ include real _________, personal _________ (other physical possessions), and intellectual _________ (rights over artistic creations, inventions, etc.), although the latter is not always as widely recognized or enforced.

a. Property
b. Disclosure requirement
c. Primary authority
d. Fiduciary

37. _________, also known as property, plant, and equipment (PP&E), is a term used in accountancy for assets and property which cannot easily be converted into cash. This can be compared with current assets such as cash or bank accounts, which are described as liquid assets. In most cases, only tangible assets are referred to as fixed.

a. Subledger
b. Fixed asset
c. Minority interest
d. Bankruptcy prediction

38. Book Value = Original Cost - _________

Book value at the end of year becomes book value at the beginning of next year. The asset is depreciated until the book value equals scrap value.

If the vehicle were to be sold and the sales price exceeded the depreciated value (net book value) then the excess would be considered a gain and subject to depreciation recapture.

a. AMEX
b. ABC Television Network
c. Accumulated depreciation
d. AIG

39. _________ are formal bookkeeping and accounting terms. They are the most fundamental concepts in accounting, representing the two records that one party in a transaction makes on its records, transferring a money balance from one account to another, one representing a reduction of liability or increase in asset, and the other representing a balancing increase in liability or reduction of asset.

Debits and credits are a system of notation used in accounting to keep track of money movements (transactions) into and out of an account.

a. Debit and credit
b. Bookkeeping
c. Cookie jar accounting
d. Controlling account

40. The basic _________ is the foundation for the double-entry bookkeeping system. It shows how assets were financed: either by borrowing money from someone (liability) or by paying your own money (shareholders' equity.)

Assets = Liabilities + (Shareholders or Owners equity)

For example: A student buys a computer for $945.

a. AIG
b. ABC Television Network
c. AMEX
d. Accounting equation

41. In accounting, _________ or carrying value is the value of an asset according to its balance sheet account balance. For assets, the value is based on the original cost of the asset less any depreciation, amortization or impairment costs made against the asset. Traditionally, a company's _________ is its total assets minus intangible assets and liabilities.

a. Generally accepted accounting principles
b. Depreciation
c. Book value
d. Matching principle

42. _________, in accrual accounting, (e.g. advance payment received from a client) is, according to revenue recognition, revenue not earned until the delivery of goods or services, which until then, is still owed to the payer, hence remaining a liability.

_________, sometimes referred to as deferred revenue or unearned revenue, shares characteristics with accrued expense with the difference that a liability to be covered latter is cash received FROM a counterpart, while goods or services are to be delivered in a latter period, when such income item is earned, the related revenue item is recognized, and the same amount is deducted from deferred revenues.

a. Deferred income
b. Treasury stock
c. Gross sales
d. Matching principle

43. The _________ is one of the basic financial statements as per Generally Accepted Accounting Principles, and it explains the changes in a company's retained earnings over the reporting period. It breaks down changes affecting the account, such as profits or losses from operations, dividends paid, and any other items charged or credited to retained earnings. A retained earnings statement is required by Generally Accepted Accounting Principles whenever comparative balance sheets and income statements are presented.

a. Notes to the financial statements
b. 3M Company
c. Statement of retained earnings
d. Financial statements

44. _________ are journal entries made at the end of an accounting period to transfer temporary accounts to permanent accounts. An 'income summary' account may be used to show the balance between revenue and expenses, or they could be directly closed against retained earnings where dividend payments will be deducted from. This process is used to reset the balance of these temporary accounts to zero for the next accounting period.

a. FIFO and LIFO accounting
b. Treasury stock
c. Trial balance
d. Closing entries

45. _________ are payments made by a corporation to its shareholder members. It is the portion of corporate profits paid out to stockholders. When a corporation earns a profit or surplus, that money can be put to two uses: it can either be re-invested in the business (called retained earnings), or it can be paid to the shareholders as a dividend.

a. Dividend payout ratio
b. Dividend stripping
c. Dividend yield
d. Dividends

46. A _________ has several related meanings:

- a daily record of events or business; a private _________ is usually referred to as a diary.
- a newspaper or other periodical, in the literal sense of one published each day;
- many publications issued at stated intervals, such as magazines, or scholarly academic _________s, or the record of the transactions of a society, are often called _________s. Although _________ is sometimes used, erroneously, as a synonym for 'magazine,' in academic use, a _________ refers to a serious, scholarly publication, most often peer-reviewed. A non-scholarly magazine written for an educated audience about an industry or an area of professional activity is usually called a professional magazine.

The word 'journalist' for one whose business is writing for the public press has been in use since the end of the 17th century.

Open access _________s are scholarly _________s that are available to the reader without financial or other barrier other than access to the internet itself. Some are subsidized, and some require payment on behalf of the author. Subsidized _________s are financed by an academic institution or a government information center.

a. 3M Company
b. BMC Software, Inc.
c. BNSF Railway
d. Journal

47. The term _________, derived from the distinctive T shape, is frequently used when discussing or analyzing accounting or business transactions. _________s are used to represent general ledger accounts.

Typically one or more Ts are drawn on a white board or blank piece of paper. A general ledger account name or number is then written above each T. Debit entries are recorded on the left side of the 'T' and credit entries are recorded on the right side of the 'T'.

a. 3M Company
b. BMC Software, Inc.
c. BNSF Railway
d. T account

48. _________ is the process of matching and comparing figures from accounting records against those presented on a bank statement. Less any items which have no relation to the bank statement, the balance of the accounting ledger should reconcile (match) to the balance of the bank statement.

_________ allows companies or individuals to compare their account records to the bank's records of their account balance in order to uncover any possible discrepancies.

a. Lower of Cost or Market
b. Credit memo
c. Bankruptcy prediction
d. Bank reconciliation

49. In accounting, a _________ is an asset on the balance sheet which is expected to be sold or otherwise used up in the near future, usually within one year, or one business cycle - whichever is longer. Typical _________s include cash, cash equivalents, accounts receivable, inventory, the portion of prepaid accounts which will be used within a year, and short-term investments.

On the balance sheet, assets will typically be classified into _________s and long-term assets.

a. Pro forma
b. General ledger
c. Deferred
d. Current asset

50. _________ is a business, economics or investment term that refers to an asset's ability to be easily converted through an act of buying or selling without causing a significant movement in the price and with minimum loss of value. Money, or cash on hand, is the most liquid asset. An act of exchange of a less liquid asset with a more liquid asset is called liquidation.

a. Financial instruments
b. Spot rate
c. Market liquidity
d. Transfer agent

51. _________ is that which is owed; usually referencing assets owed, but the term can also cover moral obligations and other interactions not requiring money. In the case of assets, _________ is a means of using future purchasing power in the present before a summation has been earned. Some companies and corporations use _________ as a part of their overall corporate finance strategy.

a. Debenture
b. Loan
c. Lender
d. Debt

52. The _________ is a financial ratio that measures whether or not a firm has enough resources to pay its debts over the next 12 months. It compares a firm's current assets to its current liabilities. It is expressed as follows:

$$\text{Current ratio} = \frac{\text{Current Assets}}{\text{Current Liabilities}}$$

For example, if WXY Company's current assets are $50,000,000 and its current liabilities are $40,000,000, then its _________ would be $50,000,000 divided by $40,000,000, which equals 1.25.

a. Times interest earned
b. Net Interest Income
c. Return on capital
d. Current ratio

53. _________ is a financial ratio that indicates the percentage of a company's assets are provided via debt. It is the ratio of total debt (the sum of current liabilities and long-term liabilities) and total assets (the sum of current assets, fixed assets, and other assets such as 'goodwill'.)

$$\text{Debt ratio} = \frac{\text{Total Debt}}{\text{Total Assets}}$$

or alternatively:

$$\text{Debt ratio} = \frac{\text{Total Liability}}{\text{Total Assets}}$$

For example, a company with $2 million in total assets and $500,000 in total liabilities would have a _________ of 25%

Like all financial ratios, a company's _________ should be compared with their industry average or other competing firms.

a. 3M Company
b. Profitability index
c. Debt ratio
d. Finance lease

54. _________ can be regarded as an outcome of mental processes (cognitive process) leading to the selection of a course of action among several alternatives. Every _________ process produces a final choice. The output can be an action or an opinion of choice.

a. Decision making
b. BNSF Railway
c. BMC Software, Inc.
d. 3M Company

1. _________ are formal records of a business' financial activities.

In British English, including United Kingdom company law, _________ are often referred to as accounts, although the term _________ is also used, particularly by accountants.

_________ provide an overview of a business' financial condition in both short and long term.

a. Financial statements
b. 3M Company
c. Notes to the financial statements
d. Statement of retained earnings

2. An _________ is a term used in behavioral economics to describe those types of behaviors that impose costs on a person in the long-run that are not taken into account when making decisions in the present. Classical Economics discourages government from creating legislation that targets internalities, because it is assumed that the consumer takes these personal costs into account when paying for the good that causes the _________. For example, cigarettes should be taxed because of the negative consumption externalities that they impose, such as second-hand smoke, not because the smoker harms him or herself by smoking.

a. Authorised capital
b. Inventory turnover ratio
c. Operating budget
d. Internality

3. In accounting and organizational theory, _________ is defined as a process effected by an organization's structure, work and authority flows, people and management information systems, designed to help the organization accomplish specific goals or objectives. It is a means by which an organization's resources are directed, monitored, and measured. It plays an important role in preventing and detecting fraud and protecting the organization's resources, both physical (e.g., machinery and property) and intangible (e.g., reputation or intellectual property such as trademarks.)

a. Internal control
b. Audit risk
c. Auditor independence
d. Audit committee

4. _________ is a demonstration of a process -- such as a variable, term, or object -- relative in terms of the specific process or set of validation tests used to determine its presence and quantity. Properties described in this manner must be sufficiently accessible, so that persons other than the definer may independently measure or test for them at will. An _________ is generally designed to model a conceptual definition.

a. AMEX
b. AIG
c. ABC Television Network
d. Operational definition

5. The _________ of 2002 (Pub.L. 107-204, 116 Stat. 745, enacted July 30, 2002), also known as the Public Company Accounting Reform and Investor Protection Act of 2002, is a United States federal law enacted on July 30, 2002 in response to a number of major corporate and accounting scandals including those affecting Enron, Tyco International, Adelphia, Peregrine Systems and WorldCom. The legislation establishes new or enhanced standards for all U.S. public company boards, management, and public accounting firms. It does not apply to privately held companies.

a. Lease
b. FCPA
c. Fair Labor Standards Act
d. Sarbanes-Oxley Act

6. In accounting/accountancy, _________ are journal entries usually made at the end of an accounting period to allocate income and expenditure to the period in which they actually occurred. The revenue recognition principle is the basis of making _________ that pertain to unearned and accrued revenues under accrual-basis accounting. They are sometimes called Balance Day adjustments because they are made on balance day.

a. Accrual
b. Adjusting entries
c. Accrued expense
d. Earnings before interest, taxes, depreciation and amortization

7. In business and accounting, _________ are everything of value that is owned by a person or company. It is a claim on the property your income of a borrower. The balance sheet of a firm records the monetary value of the _________ owned by the firm.

a. Assets
b. Accrual basis accounting
c. Accounts receivable
d. Earnings before interest, taxes, depreciation and amortization

8. _________ is a term used in accounting, economics and finance to spread the cost of an asset over the span of several years.

In simple words we can say that _________ is the reduction in the value of an asset due to usage, passage of time, wear and tear, technological outdating or obsolescence, depletion, inadequacy, rot, rust, decay or other such factors.

In accounting, _________ is a term used to describe any method of attributing the historical or purchase cost of an asset across its useful life, roughly corresponding to normal wear and tear.

a. General ledger
b. Depreciation
c. Current asset
d. Net profit

9. A _________ is an aspect of the tax code designed to incentivize a certain type of behavior. This may be accomplished through means including tax holidays or tax deductions.

a. Tax investigation
b. Tax cap
c. Tax incentive
d. Tax reform

10. In the technical language of the World Trade Organization (WTO) system, a _________ is used to restrain international trade in order to protect a certain home industry from foreign competition. A member may take a e;_________e; action (i.e., restrict importation of a product temporarily) to protect a specific domestic industry from an increase in imports of any product which is causing, or which is threatening to cause, serious injury to the domestic industry that produces like or directly-competitive products.

_________ measures were always available under the General Agreement on Tariffs and Trade (GATT) (Article XIX.)

a. Safeguard
b. BMC Software, Inc.
c. 3M Company
d. BNSF Railway

11. _________ also called 'Internal _________'. It is a term of financial audit, internal audit and Enterprise Risk Management. It means the overall attitude, awareness and actions of directors and management (i.e. 'those charged with governance') regarding the internal control system and its importance to the entity.

a. Control environment
b. Mainframe audit
c. SOFT audit
d. Negative assurance

12. Employment is a contract between two parties, one being the employer and the other being the _________. An _________ may be defined as: 'A person in the service of another under any contract of hire, express or implied, oral or written, where the employer has the power or right to control and direct the _________ in the material details of how the work is to be performed.' Black's Law Dictionary page 471 (5th ed. 1979.)

a. AMEX
b. AIG
c. ABC Television Network
d. Employee

13. _________ is a concept that denotes the precise probability of specific eventualities. Technically, the notion of _________ is independent from the notion of value and, as such, eventualities may have both beneficial and adverse consequences. However, in general usage the convention is to focus only on potential negative impact to some characteristic of value that may arise from a future event.

a. Discounting
b. Discount factor
c. Risk
d. Risk adjusted return on capital

14. _________ is a step in a risk management process. _________ is the determination of quantitative or qualitative value of risk related to a concrete situation and a recognized threat (also called hazard.) Quantitative _________ requires calculations of two components of risk: R, the magnitude of the potential loss L, and the probability p that the loss will occur.

a. Risk assessment
b. BMC Software, Inc.
c. 3M Company
d. BNSF Railway

15. The general definition of an _________ is an evaluation of a person, organization, system, process, project or product. _________s are performed to ascertain the validity and reliability of information; also to provide an assessment of a system's internal control. The goal of an _________ is to express an opinion on the person/organization/system (etc) in question, under evaluation based on work done on a test basis.

a. Assurance service
b. Audit regime
c. Institute of Chartered Accountants of India
d. Audit

16. Internal auditing is a profession and activity involved in helping organisations achieve their stated objectives. It does this by utilizing a systematic methodology for analyzing business processes, procedures and activities with the goal of highlighting organizational problems and recommending solutions. Professionals called _________ are employed by organizations to perform the internal auditing activity.

a. Auditing Standards Board
b. Internal Auditing
c. Auditor independence
d. Internal auditors

17. _________ is the concept of having more than one person required to complete a task. It is alternatively called segregation of duties or, in the political realm, separation of powers.

_________ is one of the key concepts of internal control and is the most difficult and sometimes the most costly one to achieve. The term _________ is already well-known in financial accounting systems. Companies in all sizes understand not to combine roles such as receiving checks (payment on account) and approving write-offs, depositing cash and reconciling bank statements, approving time cards and have custody of pay checks, etc.

a. Separation of duties
b. Salary
c. BMC Software, Inc.
d. 3M Company

18. A _________ is the person responsible for running the treasury of an organization. In A new way to pay the National Debt (1786), James Gillray caricatured Queen Charlotte and George III awash with treasury funds to cover royal debts, with Pitt handing them another moneybag.

The Treasury of a country is the department responsible for the country's economy, finance and revenue. The _________ is generally the head of the Treasury, although, in some countries (such as the U.S. or the UK) the _________ reports to a Secretary of the Treasury, or Chancellor of the Exchequer.

a. Treasurer
b. BMC Software, Inc.
c. 3M Company
d. BNSF Railway

19. An _________ is an audit professional who performs an audit on the financial statements of a company, government, individual and who is independent of the entity being audited. Users of these entities' financial information, such as investors, government agencies, and the general public, rely on the _________ to present an unbiased and independent evaluation on such entities. They are distinguished from internal auditors for two main reasons: (1) the internal auditor's primary responsibility is appraising an entity's risk management strategy and practices, management (including IT) control frameworks and governance processes, and (2) they do not express an opinion on the entity's financial statements.

a. Event data
b. Audit risk
c. External auditor
d. International Federation of Audit Bureaux of Circulations

20. An _________ or bill is a commercial document issued by a seller to the buyer, indicating the products, quantities, and agreed prices for products or services the seller has provided the buyer. An _________ indicates the buyer must pay the seller, according to the payment terms.

In the rental industry, an _________ must include a specific reference to the duration of the time being billed, so rather than quantity, price and discount the invoicing amount is based on quantity, price, discount and duration.

a. ABC Television Network
b. AIG
c. Invoice
d. AMEX

21. In finance, a _________ is a debt security, in which the authorized issuer owes the holders a debt and, depending on the terms of the _________, is obliged to pay interest (the coupon) and/or to repay the principal at a later date, termed maturity. It is a formal contract to repay borrowed money with interest at fixed intervals.

Thus a _________ is like a loan: the issuer is the borrower, the _________ holder is the lender, and the coupon is the interest.

a. Bond
b. Revenue bonds
c. Zero-coupon bond
d. Coupon rate

22. _________, commonly known as e-commerce or eCommerce, consists of the buying and selling of products or services over electronic systems such as the Internet and other computer networks. The amount of trade conducted electronically has grown extraordinarily since the spread of the Internet. A wide variety of commerce is conducted in this way, spurring and drawing on innovations in electronic funds transfer, supply chain management, Internet marketing, online transaction processing, electronic data interchange (EDI), inventory management systems, and automated data collection systems.

a. Electronic commerce
b. ABC Television Network
c. Electronic data interchange
d. AIG

23. A _________, also referred to as a note payable in accounting, is a contract where one party (the maker or issuer) makes an unconditional promise in writing to pay a sum of money to the other (the payee), either at a fixed or determinable future time or on demand of the payee, under specific terms. They differ from IOUs in that they contain a specific promise to pay, rather than simply acknowledging that a debt exists.

The terms of a note typically include the principal amount, the interest rate if any, and the maturity date.

a. BNSF Railway
b. Promissory note
c. 3M Company
d. BMC Software, Inc.

24. A _________ is a fungible, negotiable instrument representing financial value. they are broadly categorized into debt securities (such as banknotes, bonds and debentures), and equity securities; e.g., common stocks. The company or other entity issuing the _________ is called the issuer.

a. BMC Software, Inc.
b. 3M Company
c. Tracking stock
d. Security

25. A _________ is a type of bond that allows the issuer of the bond to retain the privilege of redeeming the bond at some point before the bond reaches the date of maturity. In other words, on the call dates, the issuer has the right, but not the obligation, to buy back the bonds from the bond holders at the call price. Technically speaking, the bonds are not really bought and held by the issuer but cancelled immediately.

a. Coupon rate
b. Zero-coupon
c. Catastrophe bonds
d. Callable bond

26. A loan is a type of debt. Like all debt instruments, a loan entails the redistribution of financial assets over time, between the _________ and the borrower.

In a loan, the borrower initially receives or borrows an amount of money, called the principal, from the _________, and is obligated to pay back or repay an equal amount of money to the _________ at a later time.

a. Lender
b. Loan to value
c. Credit rating
d. Debt

27. An account statement or a _________ is a summary of all financial transactions occurring over a given period of time on a deposit account, a credit card, or any other type of account offered by a financial institution.

_________s are typically printed on one or several pieces of paper and either mailed directly to the account holder's address, or kept at the financial institution's local branch for pick-up. Certain ATMs offer the possibility to print, at any time, a condensed version of a _________.

a. BMC Software, Inc.
b. 3M Company
c. Bank statement
d. BNSF Railway

28. _________ is the process of matching and comparing figures from accounting records against those presented on a bank statement. Less any items which have no relation to the bank statement, the balance of the accounting ledger should reconcile (match) to the balance of the bank statement.

_________ allows companies or individuals to compare their account records to the bank's records of their account balance in order to uncover any possible discrepancies.

a. Credit memo
b. Lower of Cost or Market
c. Bankruptcy prediction
d. Bank reconciliation

29. In economics, _________ or _________ goods or real _________ refers to factors of production used to create goods or services that are not themselves significantly consumed (though they may depreciate) in the production process. _________ goods may be acquired with money or financial _________. In finance and accounting, _________ generally refers to financial wealth, especially that used to start or maintain a business.

a. Vyborg Appeal
b. Screening
c. Disclosure
d. Capital

30. _________ refers to the computer-based systems used to perform financial transactions electronically.

The term is used for a number of different concepts:

- Cardholder-initiated transactions, where a cardholder makes use of a payment card
- Direct deposit payroll payments for a business to its employees, possibly via a payroll services company
- Direct debit payments from customer to business, where the transaction is initiated by the business with customer permission
- Electronic bill payment in online banking, which may be delivered by _________ or paper check
- Transactions involving stored value of electronic money, possibly in a private currency
- Wire transfer via an international banking network (generally carries a higher fee)
- Electronic Benefit Transfer

electronic funds transferPOS (short for _________ at Point of Sale) is an Australian and New Zealand electronic processing system for credit cards, debit cards and charge cards.

European banks and card companies also sometimes reference 'electronic funds transferPOS' as the system used for processing card transactions through terminals on points of sale, though the system is not the trademarked Australian/New Zealand variant.

Credit cards

_________ may be initiated by a cardholder when a payment card such as a credit card or debit card is used.

a. AIG
b. AMEX
c. Electronic funds transfer
d. ABC Television Network

31. _________ is a fee paid on borrowed assets. It is the price paid for the use of borrowed money , or, money earned by deposited funds .Assets that are sometimes lent with _________ include money, shares, consumer goods through hire purchase, major assets such as aircraft, and even entire factories in finance lease arrangements. The _________ is calculated upon the value of the assets in the same manner as upon money.

a. Insolvency
b. AIG
c. Interest
d. ABC Television Network

32. In finance, a _________ is the party in a loan agreement which receives money or other instrument from a lender and promises to repay the lender in a specified time.

a. BMC Software, Inc.
b. Simple interest
c. 3M Company
d. Borrower

33. A _________ is a deposit account held at a bank or other financial institution, for the purpose of securely and quickly providing frequent access to funds on demand, through a variety of different channels. Because money is available on demand these accounts are also referred to as demand accounts or demand deposit accounts.

They are meant neither for the purpose of earning interest nor for the purpose of savings, but for convenience of the business or personal client; hence they tend not to bear interest.

a. Reserve requirement
b. Variable rate mortgage
c. Prime rate
d. Transactional account

34. In economics, business, retail, and accounting, a _________ is the value of money that has been used up to produce something, and hence is not available for use anymore. In economics, a _________ is an alternative that is given up as a result of a decision. In business, the _________ may be one of acquisition, in which case the amount of money expended to acquire it is counted as _________.

a. Prime cost
b. Cost of quality
c. Cost allocation
d. Cost

35. In accounting, _________ has a very specific meaning. It is an outflow of cash or other valuable assets from a person or company to another person or company. This outflow of cash is generally one side of a trade for products or services that have equal or better current or future value to the buyer than to the seller.

a. ABC Television Network
b. Expense
c. AMEX
d. AIG

36. A _________ has several related meanings:

- a daily record of events or business; a private _________ is usually referred to as a diary.
- a newspaper or other periodical, in the literal sense of one published each day;
- many publications issued at stated intervals, such as magazines, or scholarly academic _________s, or the record of the transactions of a society, are often called _________s. Although _________ is sometimes used, erroneously, as a synonym for 'magazine,' in academic use, a _________ refers to a serious, scholarly publication, most often peer-reviewed. A non-scholarly magazine written for an educated audience about an industry or an area of professional activity is usually called a professional magazine.

The word 'journalist' for one whose business is writing for the public press has been in use since the end of the 17th century.

Open access _________s are scholarly _________s that are available to the reader without financial or other barrier other than access to the internet itself. Some are subsidized, and some require payment on behalf of the author. Subsidized _________s are financed by an academic institution or a government information center.

a. BNSF Railway
b. 3M Company
c. Journal
d. BMC Software, Inc.

37. _________ allows customers to conduct financial transactions on a secure website operated by their retail or virtual bank, credit union or building society.

_________ solutions have many features and capabilities in common, but traditionally also have some that are application specific.

The common features fall broadly into several categories

- Transactional (e.g., performing a financial transaction such as an account to account transfer, paying a bill, wire transfer... and applications... apply for a loan, new account, etc.)
  - Electronic bill presentment and payment - EBPP
  - Funds transfer between a customer's own checking and savings accounts, or to another customer's account
  - Investment purchase or sale
  - Loan applications and transactions, such as repayments

- Non-transactional (e.g., online statements, check links, cobrowsing, chat)
  - Bank statements
- Financial Institution Administration - features allowing the financial institution to manage the online experience of their end users
- ASP/Hosting Administration - features allowing the hosting company to administer the solution across financial institutions

Features commonly unique to business banking include

- Support of multiple users having varying levels of authority
- Transaction approval process
- Wire transfer

Features commonly unique to Internet banking include

- Personal financial management support, such as importing data into personal accounting software. Some _________ platforms support account aggregation to allow the customers to monitor all of their accounts in one place whether they are with their main bank or with other institutions.

a. ABC Television Network
b. Online banking
c. AMEX
d. AIG

38. A _________ is the transfer of wealth from one party (such as a person or company) to another. A _________ is usually made in exchange for the provision of goods, services or both, or to fulfill a legal obligation.

The simplest and oldest form of _________ is barter, the exchange of one good or service for another.

a. Payee
b. Payment
c. BMC Software, Inc.
d. 3M Company

39. Project _________: The project _________ is a prediction of the costs associated with a particular company project. These costs include labor, materials, and other related expenses. The project _________ is often broken down into specific tasks, with task _________s assigned to each.

a. 3M Company
b. Budget
c. BNSF Railway
d. BMC Software, Inc.

40. _________ is often a small amount of discretionary funds in the form of cash used for expenditures where it is not sensible to make the disbursement by check, because of the inconvenience and costs of writing, signing and then cashing the check.

The most common way of accounting expenditures is to use the imprest system. The initial fund would be created by issuing a check for the desired amount.

a. Petty cash
b. Fixed asset
c. Remittance advice
d. Minority interest

41. In United States banking, _________ is a marketing term for certain services offered primarily to larger business customers. It may be used to describe all bank accounts (such as checking accounts) provided to businesses of a certain size, but it is more often used to describe specific services such as cash concentration, zero balance accounting, and automated clearing house facilities. Sometimes, private banking customers are given _________ services.

a. 3M Company
b. Profitability index
c. Cash management
d. Finance lease

42. In financial accounting, a _________ or statement of financial position is a summary of a person's or organization's balances. Assets, liabilities and ownership equity are listed as of a specific date, such as the end of its financial year. A _________ is often described as a snapshot of a company's financial condition.

a. Balance sheet
b. Financial statements
c. 3M Company
d. Statement of retained earnings

43. _________ is the balance of the amounts of cash being received and paid by a business during a defined period of time, sometimes tied to a specific project. Measurement of _________ can be used

- to evaluate the state or performance of a business or project.
- to determine problems with liquidity. Being profitable does not necessarily mean being liquid. A company can fail because of a shortage of cash, even while profitable.
- to project rate of returns. The time of _________s into and out of projects are used as inputs to financial models such as internal rate of return, and net present value.
- to examine income or growth of a business when it is believed that accrual accounting concepts do not represent economic realities. Alternately, _________ can be used to 'validate' the net income generated by accrual accounting.

_________ as a generic term may be used differently depending on context, and certain _________ definitions may be adapted by analysts and users for their own uses. Common terms include operating _________ and free _________.

a. Commercial paper
b. Flow-through entity
c. Controlling interest
d. Cash flow

44. In financial accounting, a _________ is defined as an obligation of an entity arising from past transactions or events, the settlement of which may result in the transfer or use of assets, provision of services or other yielding of economic benefits in the future.

a. Liability
b. Corporate governance
c. Vested
d. False Claims Act

45. The _________ is the national, professional association of CPAs in the United States, with more than 330,000 members, including CPAs in business and industry, public practice, government, and education; student affiliates; and international associates. It sets ethical standards for the profession and U.S. auditing standards for audits of private companies; federal, state and local governments; and non-profit organizations.

Approximately 40% of its members are engaged in the practice of public accounting, in areas such as auditing, accounting, taxation, general business consulting, business valuation, personal financial planning and business technology.

a. AIG
b. Other postemployment benefits
c. American Institute of Certified Public Accountants
d. ABC Television Network

46. An _________ is a practitioner of accountancy, which is the measurement, disclosure or provision of assurance about financial information that helps managers, investors, tax authorities and other decision makers make resource allocation decisions.

The word '_________' is derived from the French 'Compter' which took its origin from the Latin 'Computare'. The word was formerly written in English as 'Accomptant', but in process of time the word, which was always pronounced by dropping the 'p', became gradually changed both in pronunciation and in orthography to its present form.

a. AMEX
b. Accountant
c. AIG
d. ABC Television Network

47. _________ is the statutory title of qualified accountants in the United States who have passed the Uniform _________ Examination and have met additional state education and experience requirements for certification as a _________. Individuals who have passed the Exam but have not either accomplished the required on-the-job experience or have previously met it but in the meantime have lapsed their continuing professional education are, in many states, permitted the designation '_________ Inactive' or an equivalent phrase. In most U.S. states, only _________s who are licensed are able to provide to the public attestation (including auditing) opinions on financial statements.

a. Chartered Accountant
b. Chartered Certified Accountant
c. Certified General Accountant
d. Certified Public Accountant

48. The _________ is a professional organization headquartered in Montvale, New Jersey consisting of over 70,000 members worldwide. The IMA is dedicated to advancing the role of the management accountant and financial manager within the business organization, and provides relevant professional certification.

The IMA awards the Certified Management Accountant (CMA) designation in the United States.

a. American Accounting Association
b. Institute of Management Accountants
c. International Accounting Standards Committee
d. Emerging technologies

49. _________ is concerned with the provisions and use of accounting information to managers within organizations, to provide them with the basis to make informed business decisions that will allow them to be better equipped in their management and control functions.

In contrast to financial accountancy information, _________ information is:

- usually confidential and used by management, instead of publicly reported;
- forward-looking, instead of historical;
- pragmatically computed using extensive management information systems and internal controls, instead of complying with accounting standards.

This is because of the different emphasis: _________ information is used within an organization, typically for decision-making.

a. Management accounting
b. Nonassurance services
c. Governmental accounting
d. Grenzplankostenrechnung

50. _________ of something is, in finance, the adding together of interest or different investments over a period of time such as atoms (1 - the act or process of accruing; 2 - the amount that accrues.) It holds specific meanings in accounting and payroll.

_________, in accounting, describes the accounting method known as _________ basis, whereby revenues and expenses are recognized when they are accrued, i.e. accumulated (earned or incurred), regardless when the actual cash is received or paid out.

a. Earnings before interest, taxes, depreciation and amortization
b. Accounts receivable
c. Assets
d. Accrual

51. _________ is a method of accounting whereby economic activities (rather than cash flow) of financial events are considered, because of two complementary principles, which (together) determine the point, at which expenses and revenues are recognized. According to revenue recognition principle, revenues are realized when earned, whether or not they are received in cash.

a. Earnings before interest, taxes, depreciation and amortization
b. Accrual
c. Accrued revenue
d. Accrual basis accounting

52. The _________ is a financial ratio that measures whether or not a firm has enough resources to pay its debts over the next 12 months. It compares a firm's current assets to its current liabilities. It is expressed as follows:

$$\text{Current ratio} = \frac{\text{Current Assets}}{\text{Current Liabilities}}$$

For example, if WXY Company's current assets are $50,000,000 and its current liabilities are $40,000,000, then its _________ would be $50,000,000 divided by $40,000,000, which equals 1.25.

a. Return on capital
b. Times interest earned
c. Net Interest Income
d. Current ratio

53. In accounting, a _________ is an asset on the balance sheet which is expected to be sold or otherwise used up in the near future, usually within one year, or one business cycle - whichever is longer. Typical _________s include cash, cash equivalents, accounts receivable, inventory, the portion of prepaid accounts which will be used within a year, and short-term investments.

On the balance sheet, assets will typically be classified into _________s and long-term assets.

a. Current asset
b. Deferred
c. Pro forma
d. General ledger

54. In accounting, _________ are considered liabilities of the business that are to be settled in cash within the fiscal year or the operating cycle, whichever period is longer.

For example accounts payable for goods, services or supplies that were purchased for use in the operation of the business and payable within a normal period of time would be _________.

Bonds, mortgages and loans that are payable over a term exceeding one year would be fixed liabilities.

a. Closing entries
b. Current liabilities
c. Payroll
d. Treasury stock

1. _________ are securities that can be easily converted into cash. Such securities will generally have highly liquid markets allowing the security to be sold at a reasonable price very quickly.This is a usual feature in real estate .

a. Marketable
b. BMC Software, Inc.
c. Tracking stock
d. 3M Company

2. In economics, the concept of the _________ refers to the decision-making time frame of a firm in which at least one factor of production is fixed. Costs which are fixed in the _________ have no impact on a firms decisions. For example a firm can raise output by increasing the amount of labour through overtime.

a. Long-run
b. BMC Software, Inc.
c. Short-run
d. 3M Company

3. A _________ is a fungible, negotiable instrument representing financial value. they are broadly categorized into debt securities (such as banknotes, bonds and debentures), and equity securities; e.g., common stocks. The company or other entity issuing the _________ is called the issuer.

a. Tracking stock
b. 3M Company
c. BMC Software, Inc.
d. Security

4. _________ is the term used to refer to the standard framework of guidelines for financial accounting used in any given jurisdiction. _________ includes the standards, conventions, and rules accountants follow in recording and summarizing transactions, and in the preparation of financial statements.

Financial accounting information must be assembled and reported objectively.

a. General ledger
b. Current asset
c. Generally accepted accounting principles
d. Long-term liabilities

5. _________ is generally understood in financial circles as the point at which revenue is recognized, typically through a transaction which involves the exchange of an asset, product, or service for cash or its equivalents.

This approach gives the accounting division a strictly objective basis for changing the books. For example, a homeowner may believe that his house has grown in value during a strong market, or fallen in value during a weak market, but until the house is actually sold for a specific price to a specific buyer, the change in value can only be estimated and is considered unrealized.

a. Realization
b. Valuation
c. Merck ' Co., Inc.
d. Total-factor productivity

6. _________ in law is the planning and desire to perform an act, to fail to do so (i.e. an omission) or to achieve a state of affairs in psychological view it may mean a different thing.

In criminal law, for a given actus reus ('guilty act'), the required element to prove _________ consists of showing mens rea (mental state, 'guilty mind'.)

The requirements for the proof of _________ in tort law are generally simpler than criminal law.

a. ABC Television Network
b. AIG
c. AMEX
d. Intent

7. A _________ is the pinnacle activity involved in selling products or services in return for money or other compensation. It is an act of completion of a commercial activity.

A _________ is completed by the seller, the owner of the goods.

a. Maturity
b. Tertiary sector of economy
c. High yield stock
d. Sale

8. In financial accounting, a _________ or statement of financial position is a summary of a person's or organization's balances. Assets, liabilities and ownership equity are listed as of a specific date, such as the end of its financial year. A _________ is often described as a snapshot of a company's financial condition.

a. Financial statements
b. Statement of retained earnings
c. 3M Company
d. Balance sheet

9. _________ is a company's financial statement that indicates how the revenue is transformed into the net income The purpose of the _________ is to show managers and investors whether the company made or lost money during the period being reported.

The important thing to remember about an _________ is that it represents a period of time.

a. AIG
b. AMEX
c. ABC Television Network
d. Income statement

10. A _________ is any one of a variety of different systems, institutions, procedures, social relations and infrastructures whereby persons trade, and goods and services are exchanged, forming part of the economy. It is an arrangement that allows buyers and sellers to exchange things. _________s vary in size, range, geographic scale, location, types and variety of human communities, as well as the types of goods and services traded.

a. Market
b. Recession
c. Market Failure
d. Perfect competition

11. _________ is the price at which an asset would trade in a competitive Walrasian auction setting. _________ is often used interchangeably with open _________, fair value or fair _________, although these terms have distinct definitions in different standards, and may differ in some circumstances.

International Valuation Standards defines _________ as 'the estimated amount for which a property should exchange on the date of valuation between a willing buyer and a willing seller in an arme;s-length transaction after proper marketing wherein the parties had each acted knowledgeably, prudently, and without compulsion.'

_________ is a concept distinct from market price, which is e;the price at which one can transacte;, while _________ is e;the true underlying valuee; according to theoretical standards.

a. Debtor
b. Sinking fund
c. Segregated portfolio company
d. Market value

12. _________ in economics and business is the result of an exchange and from that trade we assign a numerical monetary value to a good, service or asset. If Alice trades Bob 4 apples for an orange, the _________ of an orange is 4 apples. Inversely, the _________ of an apple is 1/4 oranges.

a. Transactional Net Margin Method
b. Discounts and allowances
c. Price discrimination
d. Price

13. In business and accounting, _________ are everything of value that is owned by a person or company. It is a claim on the property your income of a borrower. The balance sheet of a firm records the monetary value of the _________ owned by the firm.

a. Accrual basis accounting
b. Earnings before interest, taxes, depreciation and amortization
c. Accounts receivable
d. Assets

14. _________ is the balance of the amounts of cash being received and paid by a business during a defined period of time, sometimes tied to a specific project. Measurement of _________ can be used

- to evaluate the state or performance of a business or project.
- to determine problems with liquidity. Being profitable does not necessarily mean being liquid. A company can fail because of a shortage of cash, even while profitable.
- to project rate of returns. The time of _________s into and out of projects are used as inputs to financial models such as internal rate of return, and net present value.
- to examine income or growth of a business when it is believed that accrual accounting concepts do not represent economic realities. Alternately, _________ can be used to 'validate' the net income generated by accrual accounting.

_________ as a generic term may be used differently depending on context, and certain _________ definitions may be adapted by analysts and users for their own uses. Common terms include operating _________ and free _________.

a. Flow-through entity
b. Cash flow
c. Controlling interest
d. Commercial paper

15. In accounting, _________ has a very specific meaning. It is an outflow of cash or other valuable assets from a person or company to another person or company. This outflow of cash is generally one side of a trade for products or services that have equal or better current or future value to the buyer than to the seller.

a. ABC Television Network
b. Expense
c. AIG
d. AMEX

16. In financial accounting, a _________ is defined as an obligation of an entity arising from past transactions or events, the settlement of which may result in the transfer or use of assets, provision of services or other yielding of economic benefits in the future.

a. Vested
b. False Claims Act
c. Liability
d. Corporate governance

17. _________ is equal to the income that a firm has after subtracting costs and expenses from the total revenue. _________ can be distributed among holders of common stock as a dividend or held by the firm as retained earnings.

The items deducted will typically include tax expense, financing expense (interest expense), and minority interest. Likewise, preferred stock dividends will be subtracted too, though they are not an expense.

a. Long-term liabilities
b. Net income
c. Matching principle
d. Generally accepted accounting principles

18. The _________ is a financial ratio that measures whether or not a firm has enough resources to pay its debts over the next 12 months. It compares a firm's current assets to its current liabilities. It is expressed as follows:

$$\text{Current ratio} = \frac{\text{Current Assets}}{\text{Current Liabilities}}$$

For example, if WXY Company's current assets are $50,000,000 and its current liabilities are $40,000,000, then its _________ would be $50,000,000 divided by $40,000,000, which equals 1.25.

a. Times interest earned
b. Net Interest Income
c. Return on capital
d. Current ratio

19. In accounting, a _________ is an asset on the balance sheet which is expected to be sold or otherwise used up in the near future, usually within one year, or one business cycle - whichever is longer. Typical _________s include cash, cash equivalents, accounts receivable, inventory, the portion of prepaid accounts which will be used within a year, and short-term investments.

On the balance sheet, assets will typically be classified into _________s and long-term assets.

a. Current asset
b. Deferred
c. Pro forma
d. General ledger

20. In accounting, _________ are considered liabilities of the business that are to be settled in cash within the fiscal year or the operating cycle, whichever period is longer.

For example accounts payable for goods, services or supplies that were purchased for use in the operation of the business and payable within a normal period of time would be _________.

Bonds, mortgages and loans that are payable over a term exceeding one year would be fixed liabilities.

a. Treasury stock
b. Closing entries
c. Payroll
d. Current liabilities

21. _________ is one of a series of accounting transactions dealing with the billing of customers who owe money to a person, company or organization for goods and services that have been provided to the customer. In most business entities this is typically done by generating an invoice and mailing or electronically delivering it to the customer, who in turn must pay it within an established timeframe called credit or payment terms.

An example of a common payment term is Net 30, meaning payment is due in the amount of the invoice 30 days from the date of invoice.

a. Accrual
b. Accrued revenue
c. Adjusting entries
d. Accounts receivable

22. A _________ is a type of debt Like all debt instruments, a _________ entails the redistribution of financial assets over time, between the lender and the borrower.

a. Debenture
b. Loan to value
c. Lender
d. Loan

23. _________ represents claims for which formal instruments of credit are issued as evidence of debt, such as a promissory note. The credit instrument normally requires the debtor to pay interest and extends for time periods of 60-90 days or longer.

a. Restricted stock
b. Moving average
c. Public offering
d. Notes receivable

24. A _________, in business matters, is an entity that is controlled by a bigger and more powerful entity. The controlled entity is called a company, corporation, or limited liability company, and the controlling entity is called its parent (or the parent company.) The reason for this distinction is that a lone company cannot be a _________ of any organization; only an entity representing a legal fiction as a separate entity can be a _________.

a. 3M Company
b. BMC Software, Inc.
c. Parent company
d. Subsidiary

25. In accounting/accountancy, _________ are journal entries usually made at the end of an accounting period to allocate income and expenditure to the period in which they actually occurred. The revenue recognition principle is the basis of making _________ that pertain to unearned and accrued revenues under accrual-basis accounting. They are sometimes called Balance Day adjustments because they are made on balance day.

a. Accrued expense
b. Adjusting entries
c. Earnings before interest, taxes, depreciation and amortization
d. Accrual

26. _________ is a term used in accounting, economics and finance to spread the cost of an asset over the span of several years.

In simple words we can say that _________ is the reduction in the value of an asset due to usage, passage of time, wear and tear, technological outdating or obsolescence, depletion, inadequacy, rot, rust, decay or other such factors.

In accounting, _________ is a term used to describe any method of attributing the historical or purchase cost of an asset across its useful life, roughly corresponding to normal wear and tear.

a. Current asset
b. General ledger
c. Net profit
d. Depreciation

27. An _________ is a term used in behavioral economics to describe those types of behaviors that impose costs on a person in the long-run that are not taken into account when making decisions in the present. Classical Economics discourages government from creating legislation that targets internalities, because it is assumed that the consumer takes these personal costs into account when paying for the good that causes the _________. For example, cigarettes should be taxed because of the negative consumption externalities that they impose, such as second-hand smoke, not because the smoker harms him or herself by smoking.

a. Operating budget
b. Inventory turnover ratio
c. Authorised capital
d. Internality

28. In accounting and organizational theory, _________ is defined as a process effected by an organization's structure, work and authority flows, people and management information systems, designed to help the organization accomplish specific goals or objectives. It is a means by which an organization's resources are directed, monitored, and measured. It plays an important role in preventing and detecting fraud and protecting the organization's resources, both physical (e.g., machinery and property) and intangible (e.g., reputation or intellectual property such as trademarks.)

a. Auditor independence
b. Audit committee
c. Audit risk
d. Internal control

29. A _________ is an aspect of the tax code designed to incentivize a certain type of behavior. This may be accomplished through means including tax holidays or tax deductions.

a. Tax incentive
b. Tax reform
c. Tax investigation
d. Tax cap

30. _________ is a demonstration of a process -- such as a variable, term, or object -- relative in terms of the specific process or set of validation tests used to determine its presence and quantity. Properties described in this manner must be sufficiently accessible, so that persons other than the definer may independently measure or test for them at will. An _________ is generally designed to model a conceptual definition.

a. Operational definition
b. AIG
c. AMEX
d. ABC Television Network

31. In the technical language of the World Trade Organization (WTO) system, a _________ is used to restrain international trade in order to protect a certain home industry from foreign competition. A member may take a e;_________e; action (i.e., restrict importation of a product temporarily) to protect a specific domestic industry from an increase in imports of any product which is causing, or which is threatening to cause, serious injury to the domestic industry that produces like or directly-competitive products.

_________ measures were always available under the General Agreement on Tariffs and Trade (GATT) (Article XIX.)

a. 3M Company
b. BNSF Railway
c. BMC Software, Inc.
d. Safeguard

32. In financial accounting and finance, _________ is the portion of receivables that can no longer be collected, typically from accounts receivable or loans. _________ in accounting is considered an expense.

There are two methods to account for _________:

1. Direct write off method (Non - GAAP)

A receivable which is not considered collectible is charged directly to the income statement.

1. Allowance method (GAAP)

An estimate is made at the end of each fiscal year of the amount of _________. This is then accumulated in a provision which is then used to reduce specific receivable accounts as and when necessary.

a. Total Expense Ratio
b. Bad debt
c. 3M Company
d. Tax expense

33. In economics, business, retail, and accounting, a _________ is the value of money that has been used up to produce something, and hence is not available for use anymore. In economics, a _________ is an alternative that is given up as a result of a decision. In business, the _________ may be one of acquisition, in which case the amount of money expended to acquire it is counted as _________.

a. Cost
b. Prime cost
c. Cost allocation
d. Cost of quality

34. _________ is that which is owed; usually referencing assets owed, but the term can also cover moral obligations and other interactions not requiring money. In the case of assets, _________ is a means of using future purchasing power in the present before a summation has been earned. Some companies and corporations use _________ as a part of their overall corporate finance strategy.

a. Debenture
b. Lender
c. Debt
d. Loan

35. _________ is a method of evaluating an asset's worth when held in inventory, in the field of accounting. _________ is part of the Generally Accepted Accounting Principles that apply to valuing inventory, so as to not overstate or understate the value of inventory goods. Net realisable value is generally equal to the selling price of the inventory goods less the selling costs (completion and disposal).

a. BMC Software, Inc.
b. Revenue recognition
c. 3M Company
d. Net realizable value

36. _________ are formal bookkeeping and accounting terms. They are the most fundamental concepts in accounting, representing the two records that one party in a transaction makes on its records, transferring a money balance from one account to another, one representing a reduction of liability or increase in asset, and the other representing a balancing increase in liability or reduction of asset.

Debits and credits are a system of notation used in accounting to keep track of money movements (transactions) into and out of an account.

a. Debit and credit
b. Bookkeeping
c. Controlling account
d. Cookie jar accounting

37. A _________, also client, buyer or purchaser is the buyer or user of the paid products of an individual or organization, mostly called the supplier or seller. This is typically through purchasing or renting goods or services.

a. BNSF Railway
b. Customer
c. BMC Software, Inc.
d. 3M Company

38. _________ is a specific term used in companies' financial reporting from the company-whole point of view. Because that use excludes the effects of changing ownership interest, an economic measure of _________ is necessary for financial analysis from the shareholders' point of view

_________ is defined by the Financial Accounting Standards Board, or FASB, as 'the change in equity [net assets] of a business enterprise during a period from transactions and other events and circumstances from nonowner sources. It includes all changes in equity during a period except those resulting from investments by owners and distributions to owners.'

_________ is the sum of net income and other items that must bypass the income statement because they have not been realized, including items like an unrealized holding gain or loss from available for sale securities and foreign currency translation gains or losses.

a. BMC Software, Inc.
b. BNSF Railway
c. 3M Company
d. Comprehensive income

39. In bookkeeping, accounting, and finance, _________ are operating revenues earned by a company when it sells its products. Revenue (_________) are reported directly on the income statement as Sales or _________.

In financial ratios that use income statement sales values, 'sales' refers to _________, not gross sales.

a. Matching principle
b. Deferred
c. Historical cost
d. Net sales

40. _________ and credit are formal bookkeeping and accounting terms. They are the most fundamental concepts in accounting, representing the two records that one party in a transaction makes on its records, transferring a money balance from one account to another, one representing a reduction of liability or increase in asset, and the other representing a balancing increase in liability or reduction of asset.

Introduction

_________s and credits are a system of notation used in accounting to keep track of money movements (transactions) into and out of an account.

a. Bookkeeping
b. Debit
c. Cookie jar accounting
d. Debit and credit

41. The term _________ describes a reduction in recognized value. In accounting terminology, it refers to recognition of the reduced or zero value of an asset. In income tax statements, it refers to a reduction of taxable income as recognition of certain expenses required to produce the income.

a. Salvage value
b. Current asset
c. Payroll
d. Write-off

42. In finance, a _________ is the party in a loan agreement which receives money or other instrument from a lender and promises to repay the lender in a specified time.

a. Simple interest
b. 3M Company
c. BMC Software, Inc.
d. Borrower

43. A _________ is a party (e.g. person, organization, company, or government) that has a claim to the services of a second party. It is a person or institution to whom money is owed. The first party, in general, has provided some property or service to the second party under the assumption (usually enforced by contract) that the second party will return an equivalent property or service.

a. Payback period
b. Par value
c. Treasury company
d. Creditor

44. In economics a _________ is an entity that owes a debt to someone else. The entity may be an individual, a firm, a government, a company or other legal person. The counterparty is called a creditor.

a. Shares authorized
b. Fair market value
c. Segregated portfolio company
d. Debtor

45. _________ is a fee paid on borrowed assets. It is the price paid for the use of borrowed money , or, money earned by deposited funds .Assets that are sometimes lent with _________ include money, shares, consumer goods through hire purchase, major assets such as aircraft, and even entire factories in finance lease arrangements. The _________ is calculated upon the value of the assets in the same manner as upon money.

a. AIG
b. Interest
c. Insolvency
d. ABC Television Network

46. _________ is a life of security. It may also refer to the final payment date of a loan or other financial instrument, at which point all remaining interest and principal is due to be paid.

1, 3, 6 months _________ band can be calculated by using 30-day per month periods. For _________ bands over a year it is acceptable to use 365 day per year. For example with a Treasury Bond, its _________ is the date on which the principal is paid.

a. Maturity
b. The Goodyear Tire ' Rubber Company
c. Statements of Financial Accounting Standards No. 133, Accounting for Derivative Instruments and Hedging Activities
d. Factor

47. A loan is a type of debt. Like all debt instruments, a loan entails the redistribution of financial assets over time, between the _________ and the borrower.

In a loan, the borrower initially receives or borrows an amount of money, called the principal, from the _________, and is obligated to pay back or repay an equal amount of money to the _________ at a later time.

a. Credit rating
b. Debt
c. Lender
d. Loan to value

48. In financial accounting, a _________ or Statement of cash flows is a financial statement that shows a company's flow of cash. The money coming into the business is called cash inflow, and money going out from the business is called cash outflow. The statement shows how changes in balance sheet and income accounts affect cash and cash equivalents, and breaks the analysis down to operating, investing, and financing activities.

a. BNSF Railway
b. BMC Software, Inc.
c. 3M Company
d. Cash flow statement

49. In physics, and more specifically kinematics, _________ is the change in velocity over time. Because velocity is a vector, it can change in two ways: a change in magnitude and/or a change in direction. In one dimension, _________ is the rate at which something speeds up or slows down.

a. ABC Television Network
b. Acceleration
c. AMEX
d. AIG

50. _________ refers to any one of several methods by which a company, for 'financial accounting' and/or tax purposes, depreciates a fixed asset in such a way that the amount of depreciation taken each year is higher during the earlier years of an assete;s life. For financial accounting purposes, _________ is generally used when an asset is expected to be much more productive during its early years, so that depreciation expense will more accurately represent how much of an assete;s usefulness is being used up each year. For tax purposes, _________ provides a way of deferring corporate income taxes by reducing taxable income in current years, in exchange for increased taxable income in future years.

a. User charge
b. Indirect tax
c. Effective marginal tax rates
d. Accelerated depreciation

51. A _________ is the transfer of wealth from one party (such as a person or company) to another. A _________ is usually made in exchange for the provision of goods, services or both, or to fulfill a legal obligation.

The simplest and oldest form of _________ is barter, the exchange of one good or service for another.

a. Payee
b. BMC Software, Inc.
c. 3M Company
d. Payment

52. _________ is a business, economics or investment term that refers to an asset's ability to be easily converted through an act of buying or selling without causing a significant movement in the price and with minimum loss of value. Money, or cash on hand, is the most liquid asset. An act of exchange of a less liquid asset with a more liquid asset is called liquidation.

a. Market liquidity
b. Financial instruments
c. Transfer agent
d. Spot rate

53. _________ can be regarded as an outcome of mental processes (cognitive process) leading to the selection of a course of action among several alternatives. Every _________ process produces a final choice. The output can be an action or an opinion of choice.

a. Decision making
b. BNSF Railway
c. 3M Company
d. BMC Software, Inc.

54. In finance, the _________ or quick ratio or liquid ratio measures the ability of a company to use its near cash or quick assets to immediately extinguish or retire its current liabilities. Quick assets include those current assets that presumably can be quickly converted to cash at close to their book values.

$$\text{Quick (Acid Test) Ratio} = \frac{\text{Cash} + \text{Marketable Securities} + \text{Accounts Receivables}}{\text{Current Liabilities}}$$

Generally, the acid test ratio should be 1:1 or better, however this varies widely by industry.

a. Acid-test
b. Earnings per share
c. Inventory turnover
d. Invested capital

1. A _________, also client, buyer or purchaser is the buyer or user of the paid products of an individual or organization, mostly called the supplier or seller. This is typically through purchasing or renting goods or services.

a. BMC Software, Inc.
b. BNSF Railway
c. Customer
d. 3M Company

2. In economics, business, retail, and accounting, a _________ is the value of money that has been used up to produce something, and hence is not available for use anymore. In economics, a _________ is an alternative that is given up as a result of a decision. In business, the _________ may be one of acquisition, in which case the amount of money expended to acquire it is counted as _________.

a. Cost of quality
b. Cost
c. Prime cost
d. Cost allocation

3. _________ refers to the methods, practices and operations conducted to promote and sustain certain categories of commercial activity. The term is understood to have different specific meanings depending on the context. Merchandise is a sale goods at a store

In marketing, one of the definitions of _________ is the practice in which the brand or image from one product or service is used to sell another.

a. Merchandising
b. BMC Software, Inc.
c. Merchandise
d. 3M Company

4. A _________ is the pinnacle activity involved in selling products or services in return for money or other compensation. It is an act of completion of a commercial activity.

A _________ is completed by the seller, the owner of the goods.

a. Maturity
b. Sale
c. High yield stock
d. Tertiary sector of economy

5. _________ in economics and business is the result of an exchange and from that trade we assign a numerical monetary value to a good, service or asset. If Alice trades Bob 4 apples for an orange, the _________ of an orange is 4 apples. Inversely, the _________ of an apple is 1/4 oranges.

a. Price
b. Transactional Net Margin Method
c. Discounts and allowances
d. Price discrimination

6. _________, Gross profit margin or Gross Profit Rate can be defined as the amount of contribution to the business enterprise, after paying for direct-fixed and direct-variable unit costs, required to cover overheads (fixed commitments) and provide a buffer for unknown items. It expresses the relationship between gross profit and sales revenue.

It can be expressed in absolute terms:

Gross Profit = Revenue − Cost of Goods Sold

or as the ratio of gross profit to sales revenue, usually in the form of a percentage:

_________ Percentage = (Revenue-Cost of Goods Sold)/Revenue

Cost of goods sold includes variable costs and fixed costs directly linked to the product, such as material and labor.

a. 3M Company
b. BNSF Railway
c. BMC Software, Inc.
d. Gross margin

7. In accounting, _________ or sales profit is the difference between revenue and the cost of making a product or providing a service, before deducting overhead, payroll, taxation, and interest payments. Note that this is different from operating profit (earnings before interest and taxes.)

Net sales are calculated:

Net sales = Sales - Sales returns and allowances.

a. Capital structure
b. Commercial paper
c. Gross profit
d. Participating preferred stock

8. _________ is the amount of inventory a company have in stock at the end of this fiscal year. It is closely related with _________ Cost, which is the amount of money spent to get these goods in stock. It should be calculated at the Lower of Cost or Market.

a. AIG
b. Ending inventory
c. ABC Television Network
d. Inventory turnover ratio

9. _________ refers to a business or organization attempting to acquire goods or services to accomplish the goals of the enterprise. Though there are several organizations that attempt to set standards in the _________ process, processes can vary greatly between organizations. Typically the word e;_________e; is not used interchangeably with the word e;procuremente;, since procurement typically includes Expediting, Supplier Quality, and Traffic and Logistics (T'L) in addition to _________.

a. Free port
b. Supply chain
c. Consignor
d. Purchasing

10. Discounting is a financial mechanism in which a debtor obtains the right to delay payments to a creditor, for a defined period of time, in exchange for a charge or fee. Essentially, the party that owes money in the present purchases the right to delay the payment until some future date. The _________, or charge, is simply the difference between the original amount owed in the present and the amount that has to be paid in the future to settle the debt.

a. Discount factor
b. Risk aversion
c. Discount
d. Discounting

11. _________ is equal to the income that a firm has after subtracting costs and expenses from the total revenue. _________ can be distributed among holders of common stock as a dividend or held by the firm as retained earnings.

The items deducted will typically include tax expense, financing expense (interest expense), and minority interest. Likewise, preferred stock dividends will be subtracted too, though they are not an expense.

a. Long-term liabilities
b. Matching principle
c. Generally accepted accounting principles
d. Net income

12. In bookkeeping, accounting, and finance, _________ are operating revenues earned by a company when it sells its products. Revenue (_________) are reported directly on the income statement as Sales or _________.

In financial ratios that use income statement sales values, 'sales' refers to _________, not gross sales.

a. Deferred
b. Net sales
c. Historical cost
d. Matching principle

13. In finance, a _________ is a debt security, in which the authorized issuer owes the holders a debt and, depending on the terms of the _________, is obliged to pay interest (the coupon) and/or to repay the principal at a later date, termed maturity. It is a formal contract to repay borrowed money with interest at fixed intervals.

Thus a _________ is like a loan: the issuer is the borrower, the _________ holder is the lender, and the coupon is the interest.

a. Coupon rate
b. Revenue bonds
c. Zero-coupon bond
d. Bond

14. _________ is the value of a coin, stamp or paper money, as printed on the coin, stamp or bill itself by the minting authority. While the _________ usually refers to the true value of the coin, stamp or bill in question (as with circulation coins) it can sometimes be largely symbolic, as is often the case with bullion coins. For example, a one troy ounce (31 g) American Gold Eagle bullion coin was worth and sold for about $670 USD during 2006 market prices (as of July 17, 2006) and yet has a _________ of only $50 USD.

a. Face value
b. BNSF Railway
c. 3M Company
d. BMC Software, Inc.

15. A _________ is the transfer of wealth from one party (such as a person or company) to another. A _________ is usually made in exchange for the provision of goods, services or both, or to fulfill a legal obligation.

The simplest and oldest form of _________ is barter, the exchange of one good or service for another.

a. 3M Company
b. Payee
c. BMC Software, Inc.
d. Payment

16. In financial accounting, _________ or cost of sales includes the direct costs attributable to the production of the goods sold by a company. This amount includes the materials cost used in creating the goods along with the direct labor costs used to produce the good. It excludes indirect expenses such as distribution costs and sales force costs.

a. Reorder point
b. FIFO and LIFO accounting
c. 3M Company
d. Cost of goods sold

17. Under the average-cost method, it is assumed that the cost of inventory is based on the _________ of the goods available for sale during the period. _________ is computed by dividing the total cost of goods available for sale by the total units available for sale. This gives a weighted-average unit cost that is applied to the units in the ending inventory.

a. AIG
b. Ending inventory
c. Average cost
d. ABC Television Network

18. Under the _________, it is assumed that the cost of inventory is based on the average cost of the goods available for sale during the period. Average cost is computed by dividing the total cost of goods available for sale by the total units available for sale. This gives a weighted-average unit cost that is applied to the units in the ending inventory.

a. AMEX
b. ABC Television Network
c. AIG
d. Average-cost method

19. _________ is an acronym for First In, First Out, an abstraction in ways of organizing and manipulation of data relative to time and prioritization. This expression describes the principle of a queue processing technique or servicing conflicting demands by ordering process by first-come, first-served (FCFS) behaviour: what comes in first is handled first, what comes in next waits until the first is finished, etc.

Thus it is analogous to the behaviour of persons queueing (or 'standing in line', in common American parlance), where the persons leave the queue in the order they arrive, or waiting one's turn at a traffic control signal.

a. FIFO
b. Kanban
c. Trademark
d. Risk management

20. _________ methods are means of managing inventory and financial matters involving the money a company ties up within inventory of produced goods, raw materials, parts, components, or feed stocks. FIFO stands for first-in, first-out, meaning that the oldest inventory items are recorded as sold first. LIFO stands for last-in, first-out, meaning that the most recently purchased items are recorded as sold first.

a. Finished good
b. 3M Company
c. Reorder point
d. FIFO and LIFO accounting

21. _________ refers to the economic bonus which applies to certain accounts or investments that are, by statute, tax-reduced, tax-deferred, or tax-free. The most obvious examples are Retirement plans, but investments in many state or municipal bonds can also be exempt from certain taxes. Governments establish the tax advantaged status of these investments to encourage private individuals to contribute money when it is considered to be in the public interest.

a. Tax wedge
b. Tax competition
c. Tax cut
d. Tax advantage

22. In law, _________ refers to the process by which a company (or part of a company) is brought to an end, and the assets and property of the company redistributed. _________ can also be referred to as winding-up or dissolution, although dissolution technically refers to the last stage of _________. The process of _________ also arises when customs, an authority or agency in a country responsible for collecting and safeguarding customs duties, determines the final computation or ascertainment of the duties or drawback accruing on an entry.

a. Bankruptcy protection
b. BMC Software, Inc.
c. 3M Company
d. Liquidation

23. _________ is a political and social term from the Latin verb conservare meaning to save or preserve. As the name suggests it usually indicates support for tradition and traditional values though the meaning has changed in different countries and time periods. The modern political term conservative was used by French politician Chateaubriand in 1819.

a. Politicized issue
b. Conservatism
c. BMC Software, Inc.
d. 3M Company

24. A _________ proof is a mathematical proof that a particular theory is consistent. The early development of mathematical proof theory was driven by the desire to provide finitary _________ proofs for all of mathematics as part of Hilbert's program. Hilbert's program was strongly impacted by incompleteness theorems, which showed that sufficiently strong proof theories cannot prove their own _________

a. Monte Carlo methods
b. Consumption
c. Daybook
d. Consistency

25. _________ means the giving out of information, either voluntarily or to be in compliance with legal regulations or workplace rules.

- In Computer security, full _________ means disclosing full information about vulnerabilities.
- In computing, _________ widget
- Journalism, full _________ refers to disclosing the interests of the writer which may bear on the subject being written about, for example, if the writer has worked with an interview subject in the past.

- In law:
  - The law of England and Wales, _________ refers to a process that may form part of legal proceedings, whereby parties inform to other parties the existence of any relevant documents that are, or have been, in their control. This compares with the process known as discovery in the course of legal proceedings in the United States.
  - In U.S. civil procedure (litigation rules for civil cases), _________ is a stage prior to trial. In civil cases, each party must disclose to the opposing party the following: names of witnesses which it may use to support its side, copies of documents (or mere description of these documents) in its control which it may use to support its side, computation of damages claimed, and certain insurance information. _________ is related to, but technically prior to, the discovery stage.
  - In Company law (known as 'corporate law' in the United States), _________ refers to giving out information about public or limited companies or their officers, which might be kept secret if the company was a private company or a partnership.

- In real property transactions, _________ refers to providing to a buyer information known to the seller or broker/agent concerning the condition or other aspects of real property that would affect the property's value or desirability. These rules regarding what information must be disclosed, and whether the information must be disclosed even if a buyer does not ask, vary from one jurisdiction to the next.

a. Tax harmonisation
b. Controlled Foreign Corporations
c. Disclosure
d. Trailing

26. In mathematics, two elements x and y of a set partially ordered by a relation ≤ are said to be _________ if and only if x ≤ y or y ≤ x if and only if x < y or y < x or y = x. For example, two sets are _________ with respect to inclusion if and only if one is a subset of the other.

In a classification of mathematical objects such as topological spaces, two criteria are said to be _________ when the objects that obey one criterion constitute a subset of the objects that obey the other one .

a. Scientific Research and Experimental Development Tax Incentive Program
b. Consumption
c. Database auditing
d. Comparable

27. _________ are formal records of a business' financial activities.

In British English, including United Kingdom company law, _________ are often referred to as accounts, although the term _________ is also used, particularly by accountants.

_________ provide an overview of a business' financial condition in both short and long term.

a. Financial statements
b. Notes to the financial statements
c. 3M Company
d. Statement of retained earnings

28. In business and accounting, _________ are everything of value that is owned by a person or company. It is a claim on the property your income of a borrower. The balance sheet of a firm records the monetary value of the _________ owned by the firm.

a. Earnings before interest, taxes, depreciation and amortization
b. Accounts receivable
c. Assets
d. Accrual basis accounting

29. In accounting, _________ is the original monetary value of an economic item. In some circumstances, assets and liabilities may be shown at their _________, as if there had been no change in value since the date of acquisition. The balance sheet value of the item may therefore differ from the 'true' value.

a. Cost of goods sold
b. Bottom line
c. Historical cost
d. Matching principle

30. A _________ is any one of a variety of different systems, institutions, procedures, social relations and infrastructures whereby persons trade, and goods and services are exchanged, forming part of the economy. It is an arrangement that allows buyers and sellers to exchange things. _________s vary in size, range, geographic scale, location, types and variety of human communities, as well as the types of goods and services traded.

a. Perfect competition
b. Market
c. Recession
d. Market Failure

31. _________ is the price at which an asset would trade in a competitive Walrasian auction setting. _________ is often used interchangeably with open _________, fair value or fair _________, although these terms have distinct definitions in different standards, and may differ in some circumstances.

International Valuation Standards defines _________ as 'the estimated amount for which a property should exchange on the date of valuation between a willing buyer and a willing seller in an arme;s-length transaction after proper marketing wherein the parties had each acted knowledgeably, prudently, and without compulsion.'

_________ is a concept distinct from market price, which is e;the price at which one can transacte;, while _________ is e;the true underlying valuee; according to theoretical standards.

a. Sinking fund
b. Segregated portfolio company
c. Debtor
d. Market value

32. The term _________ or replacement value refers to the amount that an entity would have to pay, at the present time, to replace any one of its assets.

In the insurance industry, '_________' is a method of computing the value of an item insured. _________ is not market value, but is instead the cost to replace an item or structure at its pre-loss condition.

a. Time and motion study
b. Consolidated financial statements
c. Channel stuffing
d. Replacement cost

33. _________ is a company's financial statement that indicates how the revenue is transformed into the net income The purpose of the _________ is to show managers and investors whether the company made or lost money during the period being reported.

The important thing to remember about an _________ is that it represents a period of time.

a. Income statement
b. ABC Television Network
c. AIG
d. AMEX

34. An _________ is a period with reference to which United Kingdom corporation tax is charged. It helps dictate when tax is paid on income and gains. An _________ begins whenever a company comes within the corporation tax charge, and whenever an _________ ends without the company ceasing to be within the charge.

a. AIG
b. AMEX
c. Accounting period
d. ABC Television Network

35. In accounting, _________ has a very specific meaning. It is an outflow of cash or other valuable assets from a person or company to another person or company. This outflow of cash is generally one side of a trade for products or services that have equal or better current or future value to the buyer than to the seller.

a. AIG
b. Expense
c. AMEX
d. ABC Television Network

36. The _________ is an equation that equals the cost of goods sold divided by the average inventory. Average inventory equals beginning inventory plus ending inventory divided by 2.

The formula for _________:

$$\text{Inventory Turnover} = \frac{\text{Cost of Goods Sold}}{\text{Average Inventory}}$$

The formula for average inventory:

$$\text{Average Inventory} = \frac{\text{Beginning inventory+Ending inventory}}{2}$$

A low turnover rate may point to overstocking, obsolescence, or deficiencies in the product line or marketing effort.

a. Enterprise Value/Sales
b. Earnings per share
c. Inventory turnover
d. Upside potential ratio

37. _________ is the calculated approximation of a result which is usable even if input data may be incomplete or uncertain.

In statistics, see _________ theory, estimator.

In mathematics, approximation or _________ typically means finding upper or lower bounds of a quantity that cannot readily be computed precisely and is also an educated guess .

a. AMEX
b. AIG
c. ABC Television Network
d. Estimation

1. In accounting/accountancy, _________ are journal entries usually made at the end of an accounting period to allocate income and expenditure to the period in which they actually occurred. The revenue recognition principle is the basis of making _________ that pertain to unearned and accrued revenues under accrual-basis accounting. They are sometimes called Balance Day adjustments because they are made on balance day.

a. Adjusting entries
b. Earnings before interest, taxes, depreciation and amortization
c. Accrual
d. Accrued expense

2. In business and accounting, _________ are everything of value that is owned by a person or company. It is a claim on the property your income of a borrower. The balance sheet of a firm records the monetary value of the _________ owned by the firm.

a. Earnings before interest, taxes, depreciation and amortization
b. Accrual basis accounting
c. Accounts receivable
d. Assets

3. _________ is a term used in accounting, economics and finance to spread the cost of an asset over the span of several years.

In simple words we can say that _________ is the reduction in the value of an asset due to usage, passage of time, wear and tear, technological outdating or obsolescence, depletion, inadequacy, rot, rust, decay or other such factors.

In accounting, _________ is a term used to describe any method of attributing the historical or purchase cost of an asset across its useful life, roughly corresponding to normal wear and tear.

a. Depreciation
b. Current asset
c. General ledger
d. Net profit

4. _________ are defined as identifiable non-monetary assets that cannot be seen, touched or physically measured, which are created through time and/or effort and that are identifiable as a separate asset. There are two primary forms of intangibles - legal intangibles (such as trade secrets (e.g., customer lists), copyrights, patents, trademarks, and goodwill) and competitive intangibles (such as knowledge activities (know-how, knowledge), collaboration activities, leverage activities, and structural activities.) Legal intangibles are known under the generic term intellectual property and generate legal property rights defensible in a court of law.

a. ABC Television Network
b. Intangible assets
c. Overhead
d. AIG

5. _________ or land amelioration refers to investments making land more usable by humans. In terms of accounting, _________s refer to any variety of projects that increase the value of the property. Most are depreciable, but some _________s are not able to be depreciated because a useful life cannot be determined.

a. Land improvement
b. 3M Company
c. BNSF Railway
d. BMC Software, Inc.

6. The term _________, derived from the distinctive T shape, is frequently used when discussing or analyzing accounting or business transactions. _________s are used to represent general ledger accounts.

Typically one or more Ts are drawn on a white board or blank piece of paper. A general ledger account name or number is then written above each T. Debit entries are recorded on the left side of the 'T' and credit entries are recorded on the right side of the 'T'.

a. BMC Software, Inc.
b. 3M Company
c. BNSF Railway
d. T account

7. In economics, business, retail, and accounting, a _________ is the value of money that has been used up to produce something, and hence is not available for use anymore. In economics, a _________ is an alternative that is given up as a result of a decision. In business, the _________ may be one of acquisition, in which case the amount of money expended to acquire it is counted as _________.

a. Cost of quality
b. Cost allocation
c. Prime cost
d. Cost

8. _________ is any physical or virtual entity that is owned by an individual or jointly by a group of individuals. An owner of _________ has the right to consume, sell, rent, mortgage, transfer and exchange his or her _________. Important widely-recognized types of _________ include real _________, personal _________ (other physical possessions), and intellectual _________ (rights over artistic creations, inventions, etc.), although the latter is not always as widely recognized or enforced.

a. Disclosure requirement
b. Primary authority
c. Fiduciary
d. Property

9. _________, also known as property, plant, and equipment (PP&E), is a term used in accountancy for assets and property which cannot easily be converted into cash. This can be compared with current assets such as cash or bank accounts, which are described as liquid assets. In most cases, only tangible assets are referred to as fixed.

a. Subledger
b. Minority interest
c. Bankruptcy prediction
d. Fixed asset

10. A _________ estate is an ownership interest in land in which a lessee or a tenant holds real property by some form of title from a lessor or landlord.

_________ is a form of property tenure where one party buys the right to occupy land or a building for a given length of time. As lease is a legal estate, _________ estate can be bought and sold on the open market.

a. Liquidation value
b. Real Estate Investment Trust
c. 3M Company
d. Leasehold

11. A _________ is a one-time payment of money, as opposed to a series of payments made over time.

a. Lump sum
b. Manufacturing operations
c. Trade name
d. Redemption value

12. _________ refers to a business or organization attempting to acquire goods or services to accomplish the goals of the enterprise. Though there are several organizations that attempt to set standards in the _________ process, processes can vary greatly between organizations. Typically the word e;_________e; is not used interchangeably with the word e;procuremente;, since procurement typically includes Expediting, Supplier Quality, and Traffic and Logistics (T'L) in addition to _________.

a. Free port
b. Supply chain
c. Consignor
d. Purchasing

13. In economics, _________ or _________ goods or real _________ refers to factors of production used to create goods or services that are not themselves significantly consumed (though they may depreciate) in the production process. _________ goods may be acquired with money or financial _________. In finance and accounting, _________ generally refers to financial wealth, especially that used to start or maintain a business.

a. Capital
b. Disclosure
c. Vyborg Appeal
d. Screening

14. A _________ is an expenditure creating future benefits. A _________ is incurred when a business spends money either to buy fixed assets or to add to the value of an existing fixed asset with a useful life that extends beyond the taxable year. Capex are used by a company to acquire or upgrade physical assets such as equipment, property, or industrial buildings.

a. Cost of capital
b. Capital expenditure
c. 3M Company
d. BMC Software, Inc.

15. In accounting, _________ has a very specific meaning. It is an outflow of cash or other valuable assets from a person or company to another person or company. This outflow of cash is generally one side of a trade for products or services that have equal or better current or future value to the buyer than to the seller.

a. AMEX
b. ABC Television Network
c. Expense
d. AIG

16. _________ is a specific term used in companies' financial reporting from the company-whole point of view. Because that use excludes the effects of changing ownership interest, an economic measure of _________ is necessary for financial analysis from the shareholders' point of view

_________ is defined by the Financial Accounting Standards Board, or FASB, as 'the change in equity [net assets] of a business enterprise during a period from transactions and other events and circumstances from nonowner sources. It includes all changes in equity during a period except those resulting from investments by owners and distributions to owners.'

_________ is the sum of net income and other items that must bypass the income statement because they have not been realized, including items like an unrealized holding gain or loss from available for sale securities and foreign currency translation gains or losses.

a. Comprehensive income
b. 3M Company
c. BMC Software, Inc.
d. BNSF Railway

17. In accounting, _________ or carrying value is the value of an asset according to its balance sheet account balance. For assets, the value is based on the original cost of the asset less any depreciation, amortization or impairment costs made against the asset. Traditionally, a company's _________ is its total assets minus intangible assets and liabilities.

a. Depreciation
b. Matching principle
c. Generally accepted accounting principles
d. Book value

18. Book Value = Original Cost - _________

Book value at the end of year becomes book value at the beginning of next year. The asset is depreciated until the book value equals scrap value.

If the vehicle were to be sold and the sales price exceeded the depreciated value (net book value) then the excess would be considered a gain and subject to depreciation recapture.

a. AIG
b. Accumulated depreciation
c. ABC Television Network
d. AMEX

19. _________ is one of the constituents of a leasing calculus or operation. It describes the future value of a good in terms of percentage of depreciation of its initial value.

a. Residual value
b. 3M Company
c. Round-tripping
d. Net pay

20. Straight-line depreciation is the simplest and most often used technique, in which the company estimates the _________ of the asset at the end of the period during which it will be used to generate revenues (useful life), and will expense a portion of original cost in equal increments over that period. The _________ is an estimate of the value of the asset at the time it will be sold or disposed of; it may be zero. _________ is scrap value, by another name.

a. Closing entries
b. Net profit
c. Generally accepted accounting principles
d. Salvage value

21. There are several methods for calculating depreciation, generally based on either the passage of time or the level of activity (or use) of the asset.

_________ is the simplest and most often used technique, in which the company estimates the salvage value of the asset at the end of the period during which it will be used to generate revenues (useful life), and will expense a portion of original cost in equal increments over that period.

a. Current asset
b. Pro forma
c. Straight-line depreciation
d. Closing entries

22. In physics, and more specifically kinematics, _________ is the change in velocity over time. Because velocity is a vector, it can change in two ways: a change in magnitude and/or a change in direction. In one dimension, _________ is the rate at which something speeds up or slows down.

a. AMEX
b. Acceleration
c. ABC Television Network
d. AIG

23. _________ refers to any one of several methods by which a company, for 'financial accounting' and/or tax purposes, depreciates a fixed asset in such a way that the amount of depreciation taken each year is higher during the earlier years of an assete;s life. For financial accounting purposes, _________ is generally used when an asset is expected to be much more productive during its early years, so that depreciation expense will more accurately represent how much of an assete;s usefulness is being used up each year. For tax purposes, _________ provides a way of deferring corporate income taxes by reducing taxable income in current years, in exchange for increased taxable income in future years.

a. Accelerated depreciation
b. User charge
c. Indirect tax
d. Effective marginal tax rates

24. The _________ is a private, not-for-profit organization whose primary purpose is to develop generally accepted accounting principles (GAAP) within the United States in the public's interest. The Securities and Exchange Commission (SEC) designated the _________ as the organization responsible for setting accounting standards for public companies in the U.S. It was created in 1973, replacing the Accounting Principles Board and the Committee on Accounting Procedure of the American Institute of Certified Public Accountants. The _________'s mission is 'to establish and improve standards of financial accounting and reporting for the guidance and education of the public, including issuers, auditors, and users of financial information.'

The _________ is not a governmental body.

a. Financial Accounting Standards Board
b. Fannie Mae
c. Public company
d. Governmental Accounting Standards Board

25. _________ is the term used to refer to the standard framework of guidelines for financial accounting used in any given jurisdiction. _________ includes the standards, conventions, and rules accountants follow in recording and summarizing transactions, and in the preparation of financial statements.

Financial accounting information must be assembled and reported objectively.

a. General ledger
b. Current asset
c. Generally accepted accounting principles
d. Long-term liabilities

26. _________ methods are means of managing inventory and financial matters involving the money a company ties up within inventory of produced goods, raw materials, parts, components, or feed stocks. FIFO stands for first-in, first-out, meaning that the oldest inventory items are recorded as sold first. LIFO stands for last-in, first-out, meaning that the most recently purchased items are recorded as sold first.

a. 3M Company
b. FIFO and LIFO accounting
c. Finished good
d. Reorder point

27. The _________ is the current method of accelerated asset depreciation required by the United States income tax code. Under _________, all assets are divided into classes which dictate the number of years over which an asset's cost will be recovered.

Prior to the Accelerated Cost Recovery System (ACRS), most capital purchases were depreciated using a straight line technique, that allowed for the depreciation of the asset over its useful life.

a. Categorical grants
b. 3M Company
c. BMC Software, Inc.
d. Modified Accelerated Cost Recovery System

28. In financial accounting, a _________ or Statement of cash flows is a financial statement that shows a company's flow of cash. The money coming into the business is called cash inflow, and money going out from the business is called cash outflow. The statement shows how changes in balance sheet and income accounts affect cash and cash equivalents, and breaks the analysis down to operating, investing, and financing activities.

a. BNSF Railway
b. Cash flow statement
c. BMC Software, Inc.
d. 3M Company

29. _________ is the balance of the amounts of cash being received and paid by a business during a defined period of time, sometimes tied to a specific project. Measurement of _________ can be used

- to evaluate the state or performance of a business or project.
- to determine problems with liquidity. Being profitable does not necessarily mean being liquid. A company can fail because of a shortage of cash, even while profitable.
- to project rate of returns. The time of _________s into and out of projects are used as inputs to financial models such as internal rate of return, and net present value.
- to examine income or growth of a business when it is believed that accrual accounting concepts do not represent economic realities. Alternately, _________ can be used to 'validate' the net income generated by accrual accounting.

_________ as a generic term may be used differently depending on context, and certain _________ definitions may be adapted by analysts and users for their own uses. Common terms include operating _________ and free _________.

a. Commercial paper
b. Controlling interest
c. Flow-through entity
d. Cash flow

30. A _________ is the transfer of wealth from one party (such as a person or company) to another. A _________ is usually made in exchange for the provision of goods, services or both, or to fulfill a legal obligation.

The simplest and oldest form of _________ is barter, the exchange of one good or service for another.

a. BMC Software, Inc.
b. 3M Company
c. Payee
d. Payment

31. _________ is the process of increasing, or accounting for, an amount over a period of time. Particular instances of the term include:

- _________, the allocation of a lump sum amount to different time periods, particularly for loans and other forms of finance, including related interest or other finance charges.
  - _________ schedule, a table detailing each periodic payment on a loan (typically a mortgage), as generated by an _________ calculator.
  - Negative _________, an _________ schedule where the loan amount actually increases through not paying the full interest
- Amortized analysis, analyzing the execution cost of algorithms over a sequence of operations.
- _________ of capital expenditures of certain assets under accounting rules, particularly intangible assets, in a manner analogous to depreciation.
- _________

a. EBIT
b. Intangible
c. Annuity
d. Amortization

32. A _________ is a set of exclusive rights granted by a state to an inventor or his assignee for a limited period of time in exchange for a disclosure of an invention.

The procedure for granting _________s, the requirements placed on the _________ee and the extent of the exclusive rights vary widely between countries according to national laws and international agreements. Typically, however, a _________ application must include one or more claims defining the invention which must be new, inventive, and useful or industrially applicable.

a. Trust indenture
b. FLSA
c. Negligence
d. Patent

33. _________ is the value on a given date of a future payment or series of future payments, discounted to reflect the time value of money and other factors such as investment risk. _________ calculations are widely used in business and economics to provide a means to compare cash flows at different times on a meaningful 'like to like' basis.

The most commonly applied model of the time value of money is compound interest.

a. Net present value
b. 3M Company
c. Future value
d. Present value

34. A _________ is the name which a business trades under for commercial purposes, although its registered, legal name, used for contracts and other formal situations, may be another. Pharmaceuticals also have _________s, often dissimilar to their chemical names

Trading names are sometimes registered as trademarks or are regarded as brands.

a. Consumer-to-business
b. Trade name
c. Fund accounting
d. Price variance

35. A _________ or trade mark, identified by the symbols â„¢ (not yet registered) and Â® (registered), is a distinctive sign or indicator used by an individual, business organization or other legal entity to identify that the products and/or services to consumers with which the _________ appears originate from a unique source, and to distinguish its products or services from those of other entities. A _________ is a type of intellectual property, and typically a name, word, phrase, logo, symbol, design, image, or a combination of these elements. There is also a range of non-conventional _________s comprising marks which do not fall into these standard categories.

a. Risk management
b. Kanban
c. FIFO
d. Trademark

36. In financial accounting, a _________ is defined as an obligation of an entity arising from past transactions or events, the settlement of which may result in the transfer or use of assets, provision of services or other yielding of economic benefits in the future.

a. Corporate governance
b. False Claims Act
c. Vested
d. Liability

37. A _________ is any one of a variety of different systems, institutions, procedures, social relations and infrastructures whereby persons trade, and goods and services are exchanged, forming part of the economy. It is an arrangement that allows buyers and sellers to exchange things. _________s vary in size, range, geographic scale, location, types and variety of human communities, as well as the types of goods and services traded.

a. Market
b. Market Failure
c. Perfect competition
d. Recession

38. _________ is the price at which an asset would trade in a competitive Walrasian auction setting. _________ is often used interchangeably with open _________, fair value or fair _________, although these terms have distinct definitions in different standards, and may differ in some circumstances.

International Valuation Standards defines _________ as 'the estimated amount for which a property should exchange on the date of valuation between a willing buyer and a willing seller in an arme;s-length transaction after proper marketing wherein the parties had each acted knowledgeably, prudently, and without compulsion.'

_________ is a concept distinct from market price, which is e;the price at which one can transacte;, while _________ is e;the true underlying valuee; according to theoretical standards.

a. Debtor
b. Segregated portfolio company
c. Sinking fund
d. Market value

39. _________ are sometimes the same as net worth, or shareholders' equity - assets minus liabilities. The term _________ is commonly used with charities or not for profit entities. Although these entities don't make money, it is important to maintain reasonable reserves to help future growth.

a. Debtor days
b. Net assets
c. Net interest spread
d. Sortino ratio

40. In economic models, the _________ time frame assumes no fixed factors of production. Firms can enter or leave the marketplace, and the cost (and availability) of land, labor, raw materials, and capital goods can be assumed to vary. In contrast, in the short-run time frame, certain factors are assumed to be fixed, because there is not sufficient time for them to change.

a. Short-run
b. 3M Company
c. BMC Software, Inc.
d. Long-run

1. _________ is a file or account that contains money that a person or company owes to suppliers, but has not paid yet (a form of debt.) When you receive an invoice you add it to the file, and then you remove it when you pay. Thus, the A/P is a form of credit that suppliers offer to their purchasers by allowing them to pay for a product or service after it has already been received.

a. Earnings before interest, taxes, depreciation and amortization
b. Accounts payable
c. Accrual
d. Accounts receivable

2. In financial accounting, a _________ is defined as an obligation of an entity arising from past transactions or events, the settlement of which may result in the transfer or use of assets, provision of services or other yielding of economic benefits in the future.

a. Vested
b. Corporate governance
c. False Claims Act
d. Liability

3. In financial accounting, a _________ or statement of financial position is a summary of a person's or organization's balances. Assets, liabilities and ownership equity are listed as of a specific date, such as the end of its financial year. A _________ is often described as a snapshot of a company's financial condition.

a. Statement of retained earnings
b. Financial statements
c. Balance sheet
d. 3M Company

4. In finance, a _________ is a debt security, in which the authorized issuer owes the holders a debt and, depending on the terms of the _________, is obliged to pay interest (the coupon) and/or to repay the principal at a later date, termed maturity. It is a formal contract to repay borrowed money with interest at fixed intervals.

Thus a _________ is like a loan: the issuer is the borrower, the _________ holder is the lender, and the coupon is the interest.

a. Revenue bonds
b. Coupon rate
c. Zero-coupon bond
d. Bond

5. In economics a _________ is an entity that owes a debt to someone else. The entity may be an individual, a firm, a government, a company or other legal person. The counterparty is called a creditor.

a. Fair market value
b. Segregated portfolio company
c. Shares authorized
d. Debtor

6. A _________, also referred to as a note payable in accounting, is a contract where one party (the maker or issuer) makes an unconditional promise in writing to pay a sum of money to the other (the payee), either at a fixed or determinable future time or on demand of the payee, under specific terms. They differ from IOUs in that they contain a specific promise to pay, rather than simply acknowledging that a debt exists.

The terms of a note typically include the principal amount, the interest rate if any, and the maturity date.

a. BMC Software, Inc.
b. 3M Company
c. BNSF Railway
d. Promissory note

7. In economics, the concept of the _________ refers to the decision-making time frame of a firm in which at least one factor of production is fixed. Costs which are fixed in the _________ have no impact on a firms decisions. For example a firm can raise output by increasing the amount of labour through overtime.

a. BMC Software, Inc.
b. Long-run
c. 3M Company
d. Short-run

8. In finance, a _________ is a type of bond that can be converted into shares of stock in the issuing company, usually at some pre-announced ratio. It is a hybrid security with debt- and equity-like features. Although it typically has a low coupon rate, the holder is compensated with the ability to convert the bond to common stock, usually at a substantial discount to the stock's market value.

a. Coupon rate
b. Zero-coupon
c. Zero-coupon bond
d. Convertible bond

9. A _________ is the transfer of wealth from one party (such as a person or company) to another. A _________ is usually made in exchange for the provision of goods, services or both, or to fulfill a legal obligation.

The simplest and oldest form of _________ is barter, the exchange of one good or service for another.

a. BMC Software, Inc.
b. Payee
c. 3M Company
d. Payment

10. _________, is a liability with an uncertain timing or amount, but where the uncertainty is not significant enough to qualify it as a provision. An example is an unpaid obligation to pay for goods or services received FROM a counterpart, while cash for them is to be paid out in a latter accounting period when its amount is deducted from _________s.

a. Accrual basis accounting
b. Accounts receivable
c. Assets
d. Accrued expense

11. _________ are liabilities which have occurred, but have not been paid or logged under accounts payable during an accounting period; in other words, obligations for goods and services provided to a company for which invoices have not yet been received. Examples would include accrued wages payable, accrued sales tax payable, and accrued rent payable.

There are two general types of _________:

- Routine and recurring
- Infrequent or non-routine

Most companies pay their employees on a predetermined schedule. Let's say that the 'Imaginary company Ltd.' pays its employees each Friday for the hours worked that week.

a. Accrued liabilities
b. AMEX
c. AIG
d. ABC Television Network

12. In accounting/accountancy, _________ are journal entries usually made at the end of an accounting period to allocate income and expenditure to the period in which they actually occurred. The revenue recognition principle is the basis of making _________ that pertain to unearned and accrued revenues under accrual-basis accounting. They are sometimes called Balance Day adjustments because they are made on balance day.

a. Adjusting entries
b. Accrual
c. Earnings before interest, taxes, depreciation and amortization
d. Accrued expense

13. In accounting, _________ are considered liabilities of the business that are to be settled in cash within the fiscal year or the operating cycle, whichever period is longer.

For example accounts payable for goods, services or supplies that were purchased for use in the operation of the business and payable within a normal period of time would be _________.

Bonds, mortgages and loans that are payable over a term exceeding one year would be fixed liabilities.

a. Treasury stock
b. Payroll
c. Closing entries
d. Current liabilities

14. Employment is a contract between two parties, one being the employer and the other being the _________. An _________ may be defined as: 'A person in the service of another under any contract of hire, express or implied, oral or written, where the employer has the power or right to control and direct the _________ in the material details of how the work is to be performed.' Black's Law Dictionary page 471 (5th ed. 1979.)

a. ABC Television Network
b. AMEX
c. AIG
d. Employee

15. A _________ is a compensation, usually financial, received by a worker in exchange for their labor.

Compensation in terms of _________s is given to worker and compensation in terms of salary is given to employees. Compensation is a monetary benefits given to employees in returns of the services provided by them.

a. Retirement plan
b. 3M Company
c. Wage
d. BMC Software, Inc.

16. In accounting, _________ has a very specific meaning. It is an outflow of cash or other valuable assets from a person or company to another person or company. This outflow of cash is generally one side of a trade for products or services that have equal or better current or future value to the buyer than to the seller.

a. AIG
b. ABC Television Network
c. AMEX
d. Expense

17. _________ methods are means of managing inventory and financial matters involving the money a company ties up within inventory of produced goods, raw materials, parts, components, or feed stocks. FIFO stands for first-in, first-out, meaning that the oldest inventory items are recorded as sold first. LIFO stands for last-in, first-out, meaning that the most recently purchased items are recorded as sold first.

a. Reorder point
b. 3M Company
c. Finished good
d. FIFO and LIFO accounting

18. In economic models, the _________ time frame assumes no fixed factors of production. Firms can enter or leave the marketplace, and the cost (and availability) of land, labor, raw materials, and capital goods can be assumed to vary. In contrast, in the short-run time frame, certain factors are assumed to be fixed, because there is not sufficient time for them to change.

a. Long-run
b. BMC Software, Inc.
c. Short-run
d. 3M Company

19. _________ are liabilities with a future benefit over one year, such as notes payable that mature greater than one year.

In accounting, the _________ are shown on the right wing of the balance-sheet representing the sources of funds, which are generally bounded in form of capital assets.

Examples of _________ are debentures, mortgage loans and other bank loans (note: not all bank loans are long term as not all are paid over a period greater than a year, the example is bridging loan.)

a. Book value
b. Cash basis accounting
c. Gross sales
d. Long-term liabilities

20. In a company, _________ is the sum of all financial records of salaries, wages, bonuses and deductions.

A paycheck, is traditionally a paper document issued by an employer to pay an employee for services rendered. While most commonly used in the United States, recently the physical paycheck has been increasingly replaced by electronic direct deposit to bank accounts.

a. 3M Company
b. Tax expense
c. Total Expense Ratio
d. Payroll

21. A _________ is the pinnacle activity involved in selling products or services in return for money or other compensation. It is an act of completion of a commercial activity.

A _________ is completed by the seller, the owner of the goods.

a. Tertiary sector of economy
b. Sale
c. Maturity
d. High yield stock

22. In economics, business, retail, and accounting, a _________ is the value of money that has been used up to produce something, and hence is not available for use anymore. In economics, a _________ is an alternative that is given up as a result of a decision. In business, the _________ may be one of acquisition, in which case the amount of money expended to acquire it is counted as _________.

a. Prime cost
b. Cost of quality
c. Cost allocation
d. Cost

23. _________ is that which is owed; usually referencing assets owed, but the term can also cover moral obligations and other interactions not requiring money. In the case of assets, _________ is a means of using future purchasing power in the present before a summation has been earned. Some companies and corporations use _________ as a part of their overall corporate finance strategy.

a. Lender
b. Loan
c. Debenture
d. Debt

24. _________ is a specific term used in companies' financial reporting from the company-whole point of view. Because that use excludes the effects of changing ownership interest, an economic measure of _________ is necessary for financial analysis from the shareholders' point of view

_________ is defined by the Financial Accounting Standards Board, or FASB, as 'the change in equity [net assets] of a business enterprise during a period from transactions and other events and circumstances from nonowner sources. It includes all changes in equity during a period except those resulting from investments by owners and distributions to owners.'

_________ is the sum of net income and other items that must bypass the income statement because they have not been realized, including items like an unrealized holding gain or loss from available for sale securities and foreign currency translation gains or losses.

a. 3M Company
b. BNSF Railway
c. Comprehensive income
d. BMC Software, Inc.

25. _________, in accrual accounting, (e.g. advance payment received from a client) is, according to revenue recognition, revenue not earned until the delivery of goods or services, which until then, is still owed to the payer, hence remaining a liability.

_________, sometimes referred to as deferred revenue or unearned revenue, shares characteristics with accrued expense with the difference that a liability to be covered latter is cash received FROM a counterpart, while goods or services are to be delivered in a latter period, when such income item is earned, the related revenue item is recognized, and the same amount is deducted from deferred revenues.

a. Gross sales
b. Deferred income
c. Treasury stock
d. Matching principle

26. A _________, also client, buyer or purchaser is the buyer or user of the paid products of an individual or organization, mostly called the supplier or seller. This is typically through purchasing or renting goods or services.

a. BNSF Railway
b. BMC Software, Inc.
c. Customer
d. 3M Company

27. _________ that may or may not be incurred by an entity depending on the outcome of a future event such as a court case. These liabilities are recorded in a company's accounts and shown in the balance sheet when both probable and reasonably estimable. A footnote to the balance sheet describes the nature and extent of the _________.

a. Tangible
b. Headnote
c. Nonacquiescence
d. Contingent liabilities

28. The _________ is a private, not-for-profit organization whose primary purpose is to develop generally accepted accounting principles (GAAP) within the United States in the public's interest. The Securities and Exchange Commission (SEC) designated the _________ as the organization responsible for setting accounting standards for public companies in the U.S. It was created in 1973, replacing the Accounting Principles Board and the Committee on Accounting Procedure of the American Institute of Certified Public Accountants. The _________'s mission is 'to establish and improve standards of financial accounting and reporting for the guidance and education of the public, including issuers, auditors, and users of financial information.'

The _________ is not a governmental body.

a. Governmental Accounting Standards Board
b. Public company
c. Fannie Mae
d. Financial Accounting Standards Board

29. _________ is a company's financial statement that indicates how the revenue is transformed into the net income The purpose of the _________ is to show managers and investors whether the company made or lost money during the period being reported.

The important thing to remember about an _________ is that it represents a period of time.

a. AIG
b. AMEX
c. ABC Television Network
d. Income statement

30. In business and accounting, _________ are everything of value that is owned by a person or company. It is a claim on the property your income of a borrower. The balance sheet of a firm records the monetary value of the _________ owned by the firm.

a. Accounts receivable
b. Accrual basis accounting
c. Earnings before interest, taxes, depreciation and amortization
d. Assets

31. _________ is the balance of the amounts of cash being received and paid by a business during a defined period of time, sometimes tied to a specific project. Measurement of _________ can be used

- to evaluate the state or performance of a business or project.
- to determine problems with liquidity. Being profitable does not necessarily mean being liquid. A company can fail because of a shortage of cash, even while profitable.
- to project rate of returns. The time of _________s into and out of projects are used as inputs to financial models such as internal rate of return, and net present value.
- to examine income or growth of a business when it is believed that accrual accounting concepts do not represent economic realities. Alternately, _________ can be used to 'validate' the net income generated by accrual accounting.

_________ as a generic term may be used differently depending on context, and certain _________ definitions may be adapted by analysts and users for their own uses. Common terms include operating _________ and free _________.

a. Cash flow
b. Controlling interest
c. Commercial paper
d. Flow-through entity

32. _________ is equal to the income that a firm has after subtracting costs and expenses from the total revenue. _________ can be distributed among holders of common stock as a dividend or held by the firm as retained earnings.

The items deducted will typically include tax expense, financing expense (interest expense), and minority interest. Likewise, preferred stock dividends will be subtracted too, though they are not an expense.

a. Generally accepted accounting principles
b. Long-term liabilities
c. Matching principle
d. Net income

33. A _________ is a type of bond that allows the issuer of the bond to retain the privilege of redeeming the bond at some point before the bond reaches the date of maturity. In other words, on the call dates, the issuer has the right, but not the obligation, to buy back the bonds from the bond holders at the call price. Technically speaking, the bonds are not really bought and held by the issuer but cancelled immediately.

a. Catastrophe bonds
b. Coupon rate
c. Callable bond
d. Zero-coupon

34. A loan is a type of debt. Like all debt instruments, a loan entails the redistribution of financial assets over time, between the _________ and the borrower.

In a loan, the borrower initially receives or borrows an amount of money, called the principal, from the _________, and is obligated to pay back or repay an equal amount of money to the _________ at a later time.

a. Loan to value
b. Debt
c. Credit rating
d. Lender

35. _________ is the value of a coin, stamp or paper money, as printed on the coin, stamp or bill itself by the minting authority. While the _________ usually refers to the true value of the coin, stamp or bill in question (as with circulation coins) it can sometimes be largely symbolic, as is often the case with bullion coins. For example, a one troy ounce (31 g) American Gold Eagle bullion coin was worth and sold for about $670 USD during 2006 market prices (as of July 17, 2006) and yet has a _________ of only $50 USD.

a. BMC Software, Inc.
b. Face value
c. 3M Company
d. BNSF Railway

36. _________ is a fee paid on borrowed assets. It is the price paid for the use of borrowed money , or, money earned by deposited funds .Assets that are sometimes lent with _________ include money, shares, consumer goods through hire purchase, major assets such as aircraft, and even entire factories in finance lease arrangements. The _________ is calculated upon the value of the assets in the same manner as upon money.

a. AIG
b. ABC Television Network
c. Insolvency
d. Interest

37. _________ is a life of security. It may also refer to the final payment date of a loan or other financial instrument, at which point all remaining interest and principal is due to be paid.

1, 3, 6 months _________ band can be calculated by using 30-day per month periods. For _________ bands over a year it is acceptable to use 365 day per year. For example with a Treasury Bond, its _________ is the date on which the principal is paid.

a. Statements of Financial Accounting Standards No. 133, Accounting for Derivative Instruments and Hedging Activities
b. The Goodyear Tire ' Rubber Company
c. Factor
d. Maturity

38. _________, in finance and accounting, means stated value or face value. From this comes the expressions at par (at the _________), over par (over _________) and under par (under _________).

_________ is a nominal value of a security which is determined by an issuer company at a minimum price. _________ of an equity (a stock) is a somewhat archaic concept. The _________ of a stock was the share price upon initial offering; the issuing company promised not to issue further shares below _________, so investors could be confident that no one else was receiving a more favorable issue price. This was far more important in unregulated equity markets than in the regulated markets that exist today.

a. Creditor
b. Par value
c. Net worth
d. Restructuring

39. In finance, a _________ is the party in a loan agreement which receives money or other instrument from a lender and promises to repay the lender in a specified time.
a. Borrower
b. 3M Company
c. Simple interest
d. BMC Software, Inc.

40. A _________ is a party (e.g. person, organization, company, or government) that has a claim to the services of a second party. It is a person or institution to whom money is owed. The first party, in general, has provided some property or service to the second party under the assumption (usually enforced by contract) that the second party will return an equivalent property or service.
a. Treasury company
b. Par value
c. Creditor
d. Payback period

41. _________ refers to a business or organization attempting to acquire goods or services to accomplish the goals of the enterprise. Though there are several organizations that attempt to set standards in the _________ process, processes can vary greatly between organizations. Typically the word e;_________e; is not used interchangeably with the word e;procuremente;, since procurement typically includes Expediting, Supplier Quality, and Traffic and Logistics (T'L) in addition to _________.
a. Supply chain
b. Consignor
c. Purchasing
d. Free port

42. The _________ is a financial market where participants buy and sell debt securities, usually in the form of bonds. As of 2006, the size of the international _________ is an estimated $44.9 trillion, of which the size of the outstanding U.S. _________ debt was $25.2 trillion.

Nearly all of the $923 billion average daily trading volume in the U.S. _________ takes place between broker-dealers and large institutions in a decentralized, over-the-counter market.

a. Variance
b. Demand curve
c. Convertible bond
d. Bond market

43. A _________ is defined as a certificate of agreement of loans which is given under the company's stamp and carries an undertaking that the _________ holder will get a fixed return (fixed on the basis of interest rates) and the principal amount whenever the _________ matures.

In finance, a _________ is a long-term debt instrument used by governments and large companies to obtain funds. It is defined as 'any form of borrowing that commits a firm to pay interest and repay capital.

a. Loan to value
b. Credit rating
c. Loan
d. Debenture

44. Discounting is a financial mechanism in which a debtor obtains the right to delay payments to a creditor, for a defined period of time, in exchange for a charge or fee. Essentially, the party that owes money in the present purchases the right to delay the payment until some future date. The _________, or charge, is simply the difference between the original amount owed in the present and the amount that has to be paid in the future to settle the debt.

a. Discounting
b. Risk aversion
c. Discount
d. Discount factor

45. A _________ is the transfer of an interest in property (or the equivalent in law - a charge) to a lender as a security for a debt - usually a loan of money. While a _________ in itself is not a debt, it is the lender's security for a debt. It is a transfer of an interest in land (or the equivalent) from the owner to the _________ lender, on the condition that this interest will be returned to the owner when the terms of the _________ have been satisfied or performed.

a. BNSF Railway
b. BMC Software, Inc.
c. Mortgage
d. 3M Company

46. _________ is the value on a given date of a future payment or series of future payments, discounted to reflect the time value of money and other factors such as investment risk. _________ calculations are widely used in business and economics to provide a means to compare cash flows at different times on a meaningful 'like to like' basis.

The most commonly applied model of the time value of money is compound interest.

a. Future value
b. 3M Company
c. Present value
d. Net present value

47. _________ are financial bonds that mature in installments over a period of time. In effect, a $100,000, 5-year serial bond would mature in a $20,000 annuity over a 5-year interval. Bond issues consisting of a series of blocks of securities maturing in sequence, the coupon rate can be different.

a. Household and Dependent Care Credit
b. Low Income Housing Tax Credit
c. Just-in-time
d. Serial bonds

48. Simply put, _________ is the value of money figuring in a given amount of interest for a given amount of time. For example 100 dollars of todays money held for a year at 5 percent interest is worth 105 dollars, therefore 100 dollars paid now or 105 dollars paid exactly one year from now is the same amount of payment of money with that given intersest at that given amount of time. This notion dates at least to Martín de Azpilcueta of the School of Salamanca.

a. Time value of money
b. Merck ' Co., Inc.
c. Competition law
d. Collusion

49. A _________ is any one of a variety of different systems, institutions, procedures, social relations and infrastructures whereby persons trade, and goods and services are exchanged, forming part of the economy. It is an arrangement that allows buyers and sellers to exchange things. _________s vary in size, range, geographic scale, location, types and variety of human communities, as well as the types of goods and services traded.

a. Recession
b. Market
c. Perfect competition
d. Market Failure

50. _________ in economics and business is the result of an exchange and from that trade we assign a numerical monetary value to a good, service or asset. If Alice trades Bob 4 apples for an orange, the _________ of an orange is 4 apples. Inversely, the _________ of an apple is 1/4 oranges.

a. Discounts and allowances
b. Transactional Net Margin Method
c. Price discrimination
d. Price

51. In marketing a _________ is a ticket or document that can be exchanged for a financial discount or rebate when purchasing a product. Customarily, _________s are issued by manufacturers of consumer packaged goods or by retailers, to be used in retail stores as a part of sales promotions. They are often widely distributed through mail, magazines, newspapers, the Internet, and mobile devices such as cell phones.

a. Merchandising
b. 3M Company
c. BMC Software, Inc.
d. Coupon

52. The _________ of a bond is the amount of interest paid per year expressed as a percentage of the face value of the bond. It is the interest rate that a bond issuer will pay to a bondholder.

For example if you hold $10,000 nominal of a bond described as a 4.5% loan stock, you will receive $450 in interest each year (probably in two installments of $225 each.)

a. Revenue bonds
b. Callable bond
c. Convertible bond
d. Coupon rate

53. An _________ is the price a borrower pays for the use of money they do not own, for instance a small company might borrow from a bank to kick start their business, and the return a lender receives for deferring the use of funds, by lending it to the borrower. _________s are normally expressed as a percentage rate over the period of one year.

_________s targets are also a vital tool of monetary policy and are used to control variables like investment, inflation, and unemployment.

a. AMEX
b. AIG
c. Interest rate
d. ABC Television Network

54. A _________ is a bond bought at a price lower than its face value, with the face value repaid at the time of maturity. It does not make periodic interest payments, or so-called 'coupons,' hence the term _________. Investors earn return from the compounded interest all paid at maturity plus the difference between the discounted price of the bond and its par value.

a. Premium bond
b. Callable bond
c. Municipal bond
d. Zero-coupon bond

55. _________ relates to the cost of borrowing money. It is the price that a lender charges a borrower for the use of the lender's money. _________ is different from OPEX and CAPEX, for it relates to the capital structure of a company.

a. Interest expense
b. AIG
c. Interest
d. ABC Television Network

56. _________ is the process of increasing, or accounting for, an amount over a period of time. Particular instances of the term include:

- _________, the allocation of a lump sum amount to different time periods, particularly for loans and other forms of finance, including related interest or other finance charges.
    - _________ schedule, a table detailing each periodic payment on a loan (typically a mortgage), as generated by an _________ calculator.
    - Negative _________, an _________ schedule where the loan amount actually increases through not paying the full interest
- Amortized analysis, analyzing the execution cost of algorithms over a sequence of operations.
- _________ of capital expenditures of certain assets under accounting rules, particularly intangible assets, in a manner analogous to depreciation.
- _________

a. Intangible
b. Annuity
c. EBIT
d. Amortization

57. A _________ is like a lottery bond issued by the United Kingdom government's National Savings and Investments scheme. The government promises to buy back the bond, on request, for its original price.

_________s were introduced by the government in 1956, with the aim of encouraging saving and controlling inflation, with the first bonds going on sale on 1 November of that year.

a. Revenue bonds
b. Zero-coupon bond
c. Premium Bond
d. Callable bond

58. _________ is a term used in accounting, economics and finance to spread the cost of an asset over the span of several years.

In simple words we can say that _________ is the reduction in the value of an asset due to usage, passage of time, wear and tear, technological outdating or obsolescence, depletion, inadequacy, rot, rust, decay or other such factors.

In accounting, _________ is a term used to describe any method of attributing the historical or purchase cost of an asset across its useful life, roughly corresponding to normal wear and tear.

a. Net profit
b. General ledger
c. Current asset
d. Depreciation

59. _________ are defined as identifiable non-monetary assets that cannot be seen, touched or physically measured, which are created through time and/or effort and that are identifiable as a separate asset. There are two primary forms of intangibles - legal intangibles (such as trade secrets (e.g., customer lists), copyrights, patents, trademarks, and goodwill) and competitive intangibles (such as knowledge activities (know-how, knowledge), collaboration activities, leverage activities, and structural activities.) Legal intangibles are known under the generic term intellectual property and generate legal property rights defensible in a court of law.

a. AIG
b. ABC Television Network
c. Overhead
d. Intangible assets

60. A _________ is a one-time payment of money, as opposed to a series of payments made over time.

a. Trade name
b. Redemption value
c. Manufacturing operations
d. Lump sum

61. There are several methods for calculating depreciation, generally based on either the passage of time or the level of activity (or use) of the asset.

_________ is the simplest and most often used technique, in which the company estimates the salvage value of the asset at the end of the period during which it will be used to generate revenues (useful life), and will expense a portion of original cost in equal increments over that period.

a. Closing entries
b. Straight-line depreciation
c. Current asset
d. Pro forma

62. _________ is a form of corporation equity ownership represented in the securities. It is a stock whose dividends are based on market fluctuations. It is dangerous in comparison to preferred shares and some other investment options, in that in the event of bankruptcy, _________ investors receive their funds after preferred stock holders, bondholders, creditors, etc. On the other hand, common shares on average perform better than preferred shares or bonds over time.

a. Growth investing
b. Stock split
c. Common stock
d. 3M Company

63. In finance, an _________ is a contract between a buyer and a seller that gives the buyer the right--but not the obligation--to buy or to sell a particular asset (the underlying asset) at a later time at an agreed price. In return for granting the _________, the seller collects a payment (the premium) from the buyer. A call _________ gives the buyer the right to buy the underlying asset; a put _________ gives the buyer of the _________ the right to sell the underlying asset.

a. ABC Television Network
b. AIG
c. AMEX
d. Option

64. _________ are the earnings returned on the initial investment amount.

In the US, the Financial Accounting Standards Board (FASB) requires companies' income statements to report _________ for each of the major categories of the income statement: continuing operations, discontinued operations, extraordinary items, and net income.

The _________ formula does not include preferred dividends for categories outside of continued operations and net income.

a. Earnings yield
b. Average accounting return
c. Invested capital
d. Earnings per share

65. _________ is typically a 'higher ranking' stock than voting shares, and its terms are negotiated between the corporation and the investor.

_________ usually carries no voting rights, but may carry superior priority over common stock in the payment of dividends and upon liquidation. _________ may carry a dividend that is paid out prior to any dividends being paid to common stock holders.

a. Restricted stock
b. Preferred stock
c. Cash flow
d. Gross income

66. _________ is the state or fact of exclusive rights and control over property, which may be an object, land/real estate or intellectual property. An _________ right is also referred to as title.

_________ is the key building block in the development of the capitalist socio-economic system.

a. Administrative proceeding
b. Ownership
c. ABC Television Network
d. Encumbrance

67. _________ is a financial ratio that indicates the percentage of a company's assets are provided via debt. It is the ratio of total debt (the sum of current liabilities and long-term liabilities) and total assets (the sum of current assets, fixed assets, and other assets such as 'goodwill'.)

$$\text{Debt ratio} = \frac{\text{Total Debt}}{\text{Total Assets}}$$

or alternatively:

$$\text{Debt ratio} = \frac{\text{Total Liability}}{\text{Total Assets}}$$

For example, a company with $2 million in total assets and $500,000 in total liabilities would have a _________ of 25%

Like all financial ratios, a company's _________ should be compared with their industry average or other competing firms.

a. Profitability index
b. Finance lease
c. 3M Company
d. Debt ratio

68. The _________ is a form of financial accounting system. The most common _________ is the petty cash system.

The _________ ensures that you must document how the petty cash is spent. In a petty cash system, petty cash dockets are written for each amount issued. So when all of these dockets are totalled at the end of the month and deducted from the opening petty cash float, the calculated value must agree with what is left in the petty cash float. Under the _________, only that which is recorded as spent is replenished.

a. AIG
b. ABC Television Network
c. AMEX
d. Imprest system

69. _________ is the difference between operating revenues and operating expenses, but it is also sometimes used as a synonym for EBIT and operating profit. This is true if the firm has no non-_________.

A professional investor contemplating a change to the capital structure of a firm first evaluates a firm's fundamental earnings potential (reflected by Earnings Before Interest, Taxes, Depreciation and Amortization EBITDA and EBIT), and then determines the optimal use of debt vs. equity.

a. AIG
b. ABC Television Network
c. Operating income
d. AMEX

70. _________ is often a small amount of discretionary funds in the form of cash used for expenditures where it is not sensible to make the disbursement by check, because of the inconvenience and costs of writing, signing and then cashing the check.

The most common way of accounting expenditures is to use the imprest system. The initial fund would be created by issuing a check for the desired amount.

a. Fixed asset
b. Remittance advice
c. Minority interest
d. Petty cash

71. A _________ is a contract conferring a right on one person to possess property belonging to another person (called a landlord or lessor) to the exclusion of the owner landlord. It is a rental agreement between landlord and tenant. The relationship between the tenant and the landlord is called a tenancy, and the right to possession by the tenant is sometimes called a leasehold interest.

a. Robinson-Patman Act
b. Federal Sentencing Guidelines
c. Model Code of Professional Responsibility
d. Lease

72. _________ is any physical or virtual entity that is owned by an individual or jointly by a group of individuals. An owner of _________ has the right to consume, sell, rent, mortgage, transfer and exchange his or her _________. Important widely-recognized types of _________ include real _________, personal _________ (other physical possessions), and intellectual _________ (rights over artistic creations, inventions, etc.), although the latter is not always as widely recognized or enforced.

a. Fiduciary
b. Property
c. Primary authority
d. Disclosure requirement

73. The term _________ or superannuation refers to a pension granted upon retirement. They may be set up by employers, insurance companies, the government or other institutions such as employer associations or trade unions.

a. 3M Company
b. Wage
c. BMC Software, Inc.
d. Retirement plan

74. An _________ is a lease whose term is short compared to the useful life of the asset or piece of equipment (an airliner, a ship etc.) being leased. An _________ is commonly used to acquire equipment on a relatively short-term basis.

a. Operating lease
b. Employee Retirement Income Security Act
c. Issued shares
d. Express warranty

75. _________ is the price at which an asset would trade in a competitive Walrasian auction setting. _________ is often used interchangeably with open _________, fair value or fair _________, although these terms have distinct definitions in different standards, and may differ in some circumstances.

International Valuation Standards defines _________ as 'the estimated amount for which a property should exchange on the date of valuation between a willing buyer and a willing seller in an arme;s-length transaction after proper marketing wherein the parties had each acted knowledgeably, prudently, and without compulsion.'

_________ is a concept distinct from market price, which is e;the price at which one can transacte;, while _________ is e;the true underlying valuee; according to theoretical standards.

a. Debtor
b. Segregated portfolio company
c. Sinking fund
d. Market value

76. _________, also called fair price (in a commonplace conflation of the two distinct concepts), is a concept used in finance and economics, defined as a rational and unbiased estimate of the potential market price of a good, service, or asset, taking into account such objective factors as:

- acquisition/production/distribution costs, replacement costs, or costs of close substitutes
- actual utility at a given level of development of social productive capability
- supply vs. demand

and subjective factors such as

- risk characteristics
- cost of capital
- individually perceived utility

In accounting, _________ is used as an estimate of the market value of an asset (or liability) for which a market price cannot be determined (usually because there is no established market for the asset.) Under GAAP (FAS 157), _________ is the amount at which the asset could be bought or sold in a current transaction between willing parties, or transferred to an equivalent party, other than in a liquidation sale. This is used for assets whose carrying value is based on mark-to-market valuations; for assets carried at historical cost, the _________ of the asset is not used. One example of where _________ is an issue is a College kitchen with a cost of $2 million which was built 5 years ago.

a. BMC Software, Inc.
b. Fair value
c. BNSF Railway
d. 3M Company

77. In financial accounting, a _________ or Statement of cash flows is a financial statement that shows a company's flow of cash. The money coming into the business is called cash inflow, and money going out from the business is called cash outflow. The statement shows how changes in balance sheet and income accounts affect cash and cash equivalents, and breaks the analysis down to operating, investing, and financing activities.

a. 3M Company
b. BMC Software, Inc.
c. BNSF Railway
d. Cash flow statement

78. _________ is a term in both law and accounting that is based on the economics term of 'market value.' It is also a common basis for assessing damages to be awarded for the loss of or damage to the property, generally in a claim under tort or a contract of insurance.

A _________ is often an estimate of what a willing buyer would pay to a willing seller, both in a free market, for an asset or any piece of property. If such a transaction actually occurs, then the actual transaction price is usually the _________.

a. Disposal tax effect
b. Cash and cash equivalents
c. Shares authorized
d. Fair market value

1. A _________ is a body of elected or appointed members who jointly oversee the activities of a company or organization. The body sometimes has a different name, such as board of trustees, board of governors, board of managers, or executive board. It is often simply referred to as 'the board.'

A board's activities are determined by the powers, duties, and responsibilities delegated to it or conferred on it by an authority outside itself.

a. Consumer protection laws
b. Chief Financial Officers Act of 1990
c. Hospital Survey and Construction Act
d. Board of directors

2. _________ are payments made by a corporation to its shareholder members. It is the portion of corporate profits paid out to stockholders. When a corporation earns a profit or surplus, that money can be put to two uses: it can either be re-invested in the business (called retained earnings), or it can be paid to the shareholders as a dividend.

a. Dividend yield
b. Dividend payout ratio
c. Dividend stripping
d. Dividends

3. _________ methods are means of managing inventory and financial matters involving the money a company ties up within inventory of produced goods, raw materials, parts, components, or feed stocks. FIFO stands for first-in, first-out, meaning that the oldest inventory items are recorded as sold first. LIFO stands for last-in, first-out, meaning that the most recently purchased items are recorded as sold first.

a. Reorder point
b. Finished good
c. 3M Company
d. FIFO and LIFO accounting

4. In financial accounting, a _________ is defined as an obligation of an entity arising from past transactions or events, the settlement of which may result in the transfer or use of assets, provision of services or other yielding of economic benefits in the future.

a. Vested
b. False Claims Act
c. Liability
d. Corporate governance

5. _________ is a concept whereby a person's financial liability is limited to a fixed sum, most commonly the value of a person's investment in a company or partnership with _________. A shareholder in a limited company is not personally liable for any of the debts of the company, other than for the value of his investment in that company. The same is true for the members of a _________ partnership and the limited partners in a limited partnership.

a. Joint venture
b. Due diligence
c. Burden of proof
d. Limited liability

6. _________ is the state or fact of exclusive rights and control over property, which may be an object, land/real estate or intellectual property. An _________ right is also referred to as title.

_________ is the key building block in the development of the capitalist socio-economic system.

a. ABC Television Network
b. Administrative proceeding
c. Encumbrance
d. Ownership

7. A mutual shareholder or _________ is an individual or company (including a corporation) that legally owns one or more shares of stock in a joint stock company. A company's shareholders collectively own that company. Thus, the typical goal of such companies is to enhance shareholder value.

a. 3M Company
b. Stockholder
c. Stock split
d. Growth investing

8. In economics, business, retail, and accounting, a _________ is the value of money that has been used up to produce something, and hence is not available for use anymore. In economics, a _________ is an alternative that is given up as a result of a decision. In business, the _________ may be one of acquisition, in which case the amount of money expended to acquire it is counted as _________.

a. Cost allocation
b. Prime cost
c. Cost of quality
d. Cost

9. _________ is that which is owed; usually referencing assets owed, but the term can also cover moral obligations and other interactions not requiring money. In the case of assets, _________ is a means of using future purchasing power in the present before a summation has been earned. Some companies and corporations use _________ as a part of their overall corporate finance strategy.

a. Debt
b. Debenture
c. Lender
d. Loan

10. _________ is the process of matching and comparing figures from accounting records against those presented on a bank statement. Less any items which have no relation to the bank statement, the balance of the accounting ledger should reconcile (match) to the balance of the bank statement.

_________ allows companies or individuals to compare their account records to the bank's records of their account balance in order to uncover any possible discrepancies.

a. Bank reconciliation
b. Lower of Cost or Market
c. Bankruptcy prediction
d. Credit memo

11. A _________ or chief executive is one of the highest-ranking corporate officer (executive) or administrator in charge of total management. An individual selected as President and _________ of a corporation, company, organization, or agency, reports to the board of directors. In internal communication and press releases, many companies capitalize the term and those of other high positions, even when they are not proper nouns.

a. Return on equity
b. Return on assets
c. Kohlberg Kravis Roberts ' Co
d. Chief executive officer

12. The _________ of a company or public agency is the corporate officer primarily responsible for managing the financial risks of the business or agency. This officer is also responsible for financial planning and record-keeping, as well as financial reporting to higher management. (In recent years, however, the role has expanded to encompass communicating financial performance and forecasts to the analyst community.)

a. Chief executive officer
b. NASDAQ
c. Chief financial officer
d. Merck ' Co., Inc.

13. _________ is the imposition of two or more taxes on the same income (in the case of income taxes), asset (in the case of capital taxes), or financial transaction (in the case of sales taxes.) It refers to two distinct situations:

- taxation of dividend income without relief or credit for taxes paid by the company paying the dividend on the income from which the dividend is paid. This arises in the so-called 'classical' system of corporate taxation, used in the United States.
- taxation by two or more countries of the same income, asset or transaction, for example income paid by an entity of one country to a resident of a different country. The double liability is often mitigated by tax treaties between countries.

It is not unusual for a business or individual who is resident in one country to make a taxable gain (earnings, profits) in another. This person may find that he is obliged by domestic laws to pay tax on that gain locally and pay again in the country in which the gain was made. Since this is inequitable, many nations make bilateral _________ agreements with each other.

a. Federal Unemployment Tax Act
b. Double taxation
c. Tax shelter
d. Carbon tax

14. Simply put, _________ is the value of money figuring in a given amount of interest for a given amount of time. For example 100 dollars of todays money held for a year at 5 percent interest is worth 105 dollars, therefore 100 dollars paid now or 105 dollars paid exactly one year from now is the same amount of payment of money with that given intersest at that given amount of time. This notion dates at least to Martín de Azpilcueta of the School of Salamanca.

a. Time value of money
b. Merck ' Co., Inc.
c. Competition law
d. Collusion

15. An _________ is a tax levied on the financial income of people, corporations, or other legal entities. Various _________ systems exist, with varying degrees of tax incidence. Income taxation can be progressive, proportional, or regressive.

a. Ordinary income
b. Individual Retirement Arrangement
c. Implied level of government service
d. Income tax

16. In law, _________ refers to the process by which a company (or part of a company) is brought to an end, and the assets and property of the company redistributed. _________ can also be referred to as winding-up or dissolution, although dissolution technically refers to the last stage of _________. The process of _________ also arises when customs, an authority or agency in a country responsible for collecting and safeguarding customs duties, determines the final computation or ascertainment of the duties or drawback accruing on an entry.

a. 3M Company
b. Liquidation
c. BMC Software, Inc.
d. Bankruptcy protection

17. A _________ is a right to acquire certain property in preference to any other person. It usually refers to property newly coming into existence. A right to acquire existing property in preference to any other person is usually referred to as a right of first refusal.

In practice, the most common form of _________ is the right of existing shareholders to acquire newly issued shares issued by a company in a rights issue, a usually but not always public offering.

a. Pre-emption right
b. Fiduciary
c. Disclosure requirement
d. Corporate governance

18. In economics, _________ or _________ goods or real _________ refers to factors of production used to create goods or services that are not themselves significantly consumed (though they may depreciate) in the production process. _________ goods may be acquired with money or financial _________. In finance and accounting, _________ generally refers to financial wealth, especially that used to start or maintain a business.

a. Screening
b. Disclosure
c. Vyborg Appeal
d. Capital

19. _________ is a form of corporation equity ownership represented in the securities. It is a stock whose dividends are based on market fluctuations. It is dangerous in comparison to preferred shares and some other investment options, in that in the event of bankruptcy, _________ investors receive their funds after preferred stock holders, bondholders, creditors, etc. On the other hand, common shares on average perform better than preferred shares or bonds over time.

a. Common stock
b. Stock split
c. 3M Company
d. Growth investing

20. _________ is a specific term used in companies' financial reporting from the company-whole point of view. Because that use excludes the effects of changing ownership interest, an economic measure of _________ is necessary for financial analysis from the shareholders' point of view

_________ is defined by the Financial Accounting Standards Board, or FASB, as 'the change in equity [net assets] of a business enterprise during a period from transactions and other events and circumstances from nonowner sources. It includes all changes in equity during a period except those resulting from investments by owners and distributions to owners.'

_________ is the sum of net income and other items that must bypass the income statement because they have not been realized, including items like an unrealized holding gain or loss from available for sale securities and foreign currency translation gains or losses.

a. BNSF Railway
b. 3M Company
c. BMC Software, Inc.
d. Comprehensive income

21. _________ is typically a 'higher ranking' stock than voting shares, and its terms are negotiated between the corporation and the investor.

_________ usually carries no voting rights, but may carry superior priority over common stock in the payment of dividends and upon liquidation. _________ may carry a dividend that is paid out prior to any dividends being paid to common stock holders.

a. Restricted stock
b. Cash flow
c. Preferred stock
d. Gross income

22. In corporate law, a _________ is a legal document that certifies ownership of a specific number of stock shares in a corporation. In large corporations, buying shares does not always lead to a _________

Usually only shareholders with _________s can vote in a shareholders' general meeting.

a. BMC Software, Inc.
b. 3M Company
c. BNSF Railway
d. Stock certificate

23. In business and accounting, _________ are everything of value that is owned by a person or company. It is a claim on the property your income of a borrower. The balance sheet of a firm records the monetary value of the _________ owned by the firm.

a. Accrual basis accounting
b. Earnings before interest, taxes, depreciation and amortization
c. Accounts receivable
d. Assets

24. _________ is a fee paid on borrowed assets. It is the price paid for the use of borrowed money , or, money earned by deposited funds .Assets that are sometimes lent with _________ include money, shares, consumer goods through hire purchase, major assets such as aircraft, and even entire factories in finance lease arrangements. The _________ is calculated upon the value of the assets in the same manner as upon money.

a. Insolvency
b. ABC Television Network
c. AIG
d. Interest

25. _________ are common shares that have been authorized, issued, and purchased by investors. They have voting rights and represent ownership in the corporation by the person or institution that holds the shares. They should be distinguished from treasury shares, which are common stock repurchased by the corporation.

a. Shares outstanding
b. Controlling interest
c. Participating preferred stock
d. Preferred stock

26. _________, in finance and accounting, means stated value or face value. From this comes the expressions at par (at the _________), over par (over _________) and under par (under _________).

_________ is a nominal value of a security which is determined by an issuer company at a minimum price. _________ of an equity (a stock) is a somewhat archaic concept. The _________ of a stock was the share price upon initial offering; the issuing company promised not to issue further shares below _________, so investors could be confident that no one else was receiving a more favorable issue price. This was far more important in unregulated equity markets than in the regulated markets that exist today.

a. Par value
b. Net worth
c. Restructuring
d. Creditor

27. Initial _________, also referred to simply as a '_________' or 'flotation,' is when a company issues common stock or shares to the public for the first time. They are often issued by smaller, younger companies seeking capital to expand, but can also be done by large privately-owned companies looking to become publicly traded.

In an Ipublic offering the issuer may obtain the assistance of an underwriting firm, which helps it determine what type of security to issue (common or preferred), best offering price and time to bring it to market.

a. Gross income
b. Commercial paper
c. Restricted stock
d. Public offering

28. In finance, a _________ is a debt security, in which the authorized issuer owes the holders a debt and, depending on the terms of the _________, is obliged to pay interest (the coupon) and/or to repay the principal at a later date, termed maturity. It is a formal contract to repay borrowed money with interest at fixed intervals.

Thus a _________ is like a loan: the issuer is the borrower, the _________ holder is the lender, and the coupon is the interest.

a. Revenue bonds
b. Coupon rate
c. Zero-coupon bond
d. Bond

29. A _________ is a party (e.g. person, organization, company, or government) that has a claim to the services of a second party. It is a person or institution to whom money is owed. The first party, in general, has provided some property or service to the second party under the assumption (usually enforced by contract) that the second party will return an equivalent property or service.

a. Payback period
b. Treasury company
c. Creditor
d. Par value

30. _________ refers to a business or organization attempting to acquire goods or services to accomplish the goals of the enterprise. Though there are several organizations that attempt to set standards in the _________ process, processes can vary greatly between organizations. Typically the word e;_________e; is not used interchangeably with the word e;procuremente;, since procurement typically includes Expediting, Supplier Quality, and Traffic and Logistics (T'L) in addition to _________.

a. Purchasing
b. Supply chain
c. Consignor
d. Free port

31. In accounting, _________ or carrying value is the value of an asset according to its balance sheet account balance. For assets, the value is based on the original cost of the asset less any depreciation, amortization or impairment costs made against the asset. Traditionally, a company's _________ is its total assets minus intangible assets and liabilities.

a. Generally accepted accounting principles
b. Matching principle
c. Depreciation
d. Book value

32. In accounting/accountancy, _________ are journal entries usually made at the end of an accounting period to allocate income and expenditure to the period in which they actually occurred. The revenue recognition principle is the basis of making _________ that pertain to unearned and accrued revenues under accrual-basis accounting. They are sometimes called Balance Day adjustments because they are made on balance day.

a. Earnings before interest, taxes, depreciation and amortization
b. Accrual
c. Accrued expense
d. Adjusting entries

33. _________ is a term used in accounting, economics and finance to spread the cost of an asset over the span of several years.

In simple words we can say that _________ is the reduction in the value of an asset due to usage, passage of time, wear and tear, technological outdating or obsolescence, depletion, inadequacy, rot, rust, decay or other such factors.

In accounting, _________ is a term used to describe any method of attributing the historical or purchase cost of an asset across its useful life, roughly corresponding to normal wear and tear.

a. General ledger
b. Depreciation
c. Current asset
d. Net profit

34. A _________ or reacquired stock is stock which is bought back by the issuing company, reducing the amount of outstanding stock on the open market ('open market' including insiders' holdings).

Stock repurchases are often used as a tax-efficient method to put cash into shareholders' hands, rather than pay dividends. Sometimes, companies do this when they feel that their stock is undervalued on the open market.

a. Net profit
b. Matching principle
c. Cost of goods sold
d. Treasury stock

35. _________, in accrual accounting, is any account where the asset or liability is not realized until a future date (accounting period), e.g. annuities, charges, taxes, income, etc. The _________ item may be carried, dependent on type of deferral, as either an asset or liability.

a. Deferred
b. Payroll
c. Pro forma
d. Cash basis accounting

36. _________, in accrual accounting, (e.g. advance payment received from a client) is, according to revenue recognition, revenue not earned until the delivery of goods or services, which until then, is still owed to the payer, hence remaining a liability.

_________, sometimes referred to as deferred revenue or unearned revenue, shares characteristics with accrued expense with the difference that a liability to be covered latter is cash received FROM a counterpart, while goods or services are to be delivered in a latter period, when such income item is earned, the related revenue item is recognized, and the same amount is deducted from deferred revenues.

a. Treasury stock
b. Deferred income
c. Gross sales
d. Matching principle

37. A _________ or stock divide increases or decreases the number of shares in a public company. The price is adjusted such that the before and after market capitalization of the company remains the same and dilution does not occur. Options and warrants are included.

a. Stockholder
b. 3M Company
c. Stock split
d. Growth investing

38. In accounting, _________ are considered liabilities of the business that are to be settled in cash within the fiscal year or the operating cycle, whichever period is longer.

For example accounts payable for goods, services or supplies that were purchased for use in the operation of the business and payable within a normal period of time would be _________.

Bonds, mortgages and loans that are payable over a term exceeding one year would be fixed liabilities.

a. Current liabilities
b. Payroll
c. Closing entries
d. Treasury stock

39. In economic models, the _________ time frame assumes no fixed factors of production. Firms can enter or leave the marketplace, and the cost (and availability) of land, labor, raw materials, and capital goods can be assumed to vary. In contrast, in the short-run time frame, certain factors are assumed to be fixed, because there is not sufficient time for them to change.

a. 3M Company
b. BMC Software, Inc.
c. Short-run
d. Long-run

40. _________ are liabilities with a future benefit over one year, such as notes payable that mature greater than one year.

In accounting, the _________ are shown on the right wing of the balance-sheet representing the sources of funds, which are generally bounded in form of capital assets.

Examples of _________ are debentures, mortgage loans and other bank loans (note: not all bank loans are long term as not all are paid over a period greater than a year, the example is bridging loan.)

a. Cash basis accounting
b. Gross sales
c. Book value
d. Long-term liabilities

41. _________ is the likely price of an asset when it is allowed insufficient time to sell on the open market, thereby reducing its exposure to potential buyers. _________ is typically lower than fair market value. Unlike cash or securities, certain illiquid assets, like real estate, often require a period of several months in order to obtain their fair market value in a sale, and will generally sell for a significantly lower price if a sale is forced to occur in a shorter time period.

a. Real Estate Investment Trust
b. 3M Company
c. REIT
d. Liquidation value

42. A _________ is any one of a variety of different systems, institutions, procedures, social relations and infrastructures whereby persons trade, and goods and services are exchanged, forming part of the economy. It is an arrangement that allows buyers and sellers to exchange things. _________s vary in size, range, geographic scale, location, types and variety of human communities, as well as the types of goods and services traded.

a. Perfect competition
b. Market Failure
c. Recession
d. Market

43. _________ is an economic concept with commonplace familiarity. It is the price that a good or service is offered at, or will fetch, in the marketplace. It is of interest mainly in the study of microeconomics.

a. Spot rate
b. Market price
c. Financial instruments
d. Transfer agent

44. _________ is the price at which an asset would trade in a competitive Walrasian auction setting. _________ is often used interchangeably with open _________, fair value or fair _________, although these terms have distinct definitions in different standards, and may differ in some circumstances.

International Valuation Standards defines _________ as 'the estimated amount for which a property should exchange on the date of valuation between a willing buyer and a willing seller in an arme;s-length transaction after proper marketing wherein the parties had each acted knowledgeably, prudently, and without compulsion.'

_________ is a concept distinct from market price, which is e;the price at which one can transacte;, while _________ is e;the true underlying valuee; according to theoretical standards.

a. Segregated portfolio company
b. Sinking fund
c. Debtor
d. Market value

45. _________ in economics and business is the result of an exchange and from that trade we assign a numerical monetary value to a good, service or asset. If Alice trades Bob 4 apples for an orange, the _________ of an orange is 4 apples. Inversely, the _________ of an apple is 1/4 oranges.

a. Price discrimination
b. Transactional Net Margin Method
c. Price
d. Discounts and allowances

46. _________ is the price at which the issuing company may choose to repurchase a security before its maturity date.

A bond is purchased at a discount if its _________ exceeds its purchase price. It is purchased at a premium if its purchase price exceeds its _________.

a. Lump sum
b. Trade name
c. Consolidated financial statements
d. Redemption value

47. Book Value = Original Cost - _________

Book value at the end of year becomes book value at the beginning of next year. The asset is depreciated until the book value equals scrap value.

If the vehicle were to be sold and the sales price exceeded the depreciated value (net book value) then the excess would be considered a gain and subject to depreciation recapture.

a. Accumulated depreciation
b. ABC Television Network
c. AMEX
d. AIG

48. _________ is equal to the income that a firm has after subtracting costs and expenses from the total revenue. _________ can be distributed among holders of common stock as a dividend or held by the firm as retained earnings.

The items deducted will typically include tax expense, financing expense (interest expense), and minority interest. Likewise, preferred stock dividends will be subtracted too, though they are not an expense.

a. Matching principle
b. Generally accepted accounting principles
c. Long-term liabilities
d. Net income

49. In finance, _________ also known as return on investment, rate of profit or sometimes just return, is the ratio of money gained or lost on an investment relative to the amount of money invested. The amount of money gained or lost may be referred to as interest, profit/loss, gain/loss, or net income/loss. The money invested may be referred to as the asset, capital, principal, or the cost basis of the investment.

a. Debt to capital ratio
b. Capital employed
c. Theoretical ex-rights price
d. Rate of return

50. The _________ percentage shows how profitable a company's assets are in generating revenue.

_________ can be computed as:

$$\text{ROA} = \frac{\text{Net Income - Interest Expense - Interest Tax savings}}{\text{Average Total Assets}}$$

This number tells you what the company can do with what it has, i.e. how many dollars of earnings they derive from each dollar of assets they control. Its a useful number for comparing competing companies in the same industry.

a. Return on sales
b. Statutory Liquidity Ratio
c. Capital employed
d. Return on assets

51. In accounting, _________ has a very specific meaning. It is an outflow of cash or other valuable assets from a person or company to another person or company. This outflow of cash is generally one side of a trade for products or services that have equal or better current or future value to the buyer than to the seller.

a. Expense
b. ABC Television Network
c. AMEX
d. AIG

52. _________ relates to the cost of borrowing money. It is the price that a lender charges a borrower for the use of the lender's money. _________ is different from OPEX and CAPEX, for it relates to the capital structure of a company.

a. Interest
b. AIG
c. Interest expense
d. ABC Television Network

53. _________ measures the rate of return on the ownership interest (shareholders' equity) of the common stock owners. It measures a firm's efficiency at generating profits from every dollar of shareholders' equity (also known as net assets or assets minus liabilities.) It shows how well a company uses investment dollars to generate earnings growth.

a. Sortino ratio
b. Like for like
c. Return on equity
d. Return on capital employed

54. _________ is the balance of the amounts of cash being received and paid by a business during a defined period of time, sometimes tied to a specific project. Measurement of _________ can be used

- to evaluate the state or performance of a business or project.
- to determine problems with liquidity. Being profitable does not necessarily mean being liquid. A company can fail because of a shortage of cash, even while profitable.
- to project rate of returns. The time of _________s into and out of projects are used as inputs to financial models such as internal rate of return, and net present value.
- to examine income or growth of a business when it is believed that accrual accounting concepts do not represent economic realities. Alternately, _________ can be used to 'validate' the net income generated by accrual accounting.

_________ as a generic term may be used differently depending on context, and certain _________ definitions may be adapted by analysts and users for their own uses. Common terms include operating _________ and free _________.

a. Commercial paper
b. Flow-through entity
c. Controlling interest
d. Cash flow

55. In financial accounting, a _________ or Statement of cash flows is a financial statement that shows a company's flow of cash. The money coming into the business is called cash inflow, and money going out from the business is called cash outflow. The statement shows how changes in balance sheet and income accounts affect cash and cash equivalents, and breaks the analysis down to operating, investing, and financing activities.

a. 3M Company
b. BMC Software, Inc.
c. Cash flow statement
d. BNSF Railway

56. A _________ is the transfer of wealth from one party (such as a person or company) to another. A _________ is usually made in exchange for the provision of goods, services or both, or to fulfill a legal obligation.

The simplest and oldest form of _________ is barter, the exchange of one good or service for another.

a. 3M Company
b. Payment
c. Payee
d. BMC Software, Inc.

1. In financial accounting, a _________ or statement of financial position is a summary of a person's or organization's balances. Assets, liabilities and ownership equity are listed as of a specific date, such as the end of its financial year. A _________ is often described as a snapshot of a company's financial condition.

a. Financial statements
b. 3M Company
c. Balance sheet
d. Statement of retained earnings

2. _________ is a form of corporation equity ownership represented in the securities. It is a stock whose dividends are based on market fluctuations. It is dangerous in comparison to preferred shares and some other investment options, in that in the event of bankruptcy, _________ investors receive their funds after preferred stock holders, bondholders, creditors, etc. On the other hand, common shares on average perform better than preferred shares or bonds over time.

a. Stock split
b. 3M Company
c. Growth investing
d. Common stock

3. In economic models, the _________ time frame assumes no fixed factors of production. Firms can enter or leave the marketplace, and the cost (and availability) of land, labor, raw materials, and capital goods can be assumed to vary. In contrast, in the short-run time frame, certain factors are assumed to be fixed, because there is not sufficient time for them to change.

a. 3M Company
b. Short-run
c. BMC Software, Inc.
d. Long-run

4. _________ is typically a 'higher ranking' stock than voting shares, and its terms are negotiated between the corporation and the investor.

_________ usually carries no voting rights, but may carry superior priority over common stock in the payment of dividends and upon liquidation. _________ may carry a dividend that is paid out prior to any dividends being paid to common stock holders.

a. Gross income
b. Restricted stock
c. Cash flow
d. Preferred stock

5. In economics, the concept of the _________ refers to the decision-making time frame of a firm in which at least one factor of production is fixed. Costs which are fixed in the _________ have no impact on a firms decisions. For example a firm can raise output by increasing the amount of labour through overtime.

a. Long-run
b. BMC Software, Inc.
c. 3M Company
d. Short-run

6. In business and accounting, _________ are everything of value that is owned by a person or company. It is a claim on the property your income of a borrower. The balance sheet of a firm records the monetary value of the _________ owned by the firm.

a. Accrual basis accounting
b. Assets
c. Accounts receivable
d. Earnings before interest, taxes, depreciation and amortization

7. _________ is the balance of the amounts of cash being received and paid by a business during a defined period of time, sometimes tied to a specific project. Measurement of _________ can be used

- to evaluate the state or performance of a business or project.
- to determine problems with liquidity. Being profitable does not necessarily mean being liquid. A company can fail because of a shortage of cash, even while profitable.
- to project rate of returns. The time of _________s into and out of projects are used as inputs to financial models such as internal rate of return, and net present value.
- to examine income or growth of a business when it is believed that accrual accounting concepts do not represent economic realities. Alternately, _________ can be used to 'validate' the net income generated by accrual accounting.

_________ as a generic term may be used differently depending on context, and certain _________ definitions may be adapted by analysts and users for their own uses. Common terms include operating _________ and free _________.

a. Controlling interest
b. Commercial paper
c. Flow-through entity
d. Cash flow

8. In financial accounting, a _________ is defined as an obligation of an entity arising from past transactions or events, the settlement of which may result in the transfer or use of assets, provision of services or other yielding of economic benefits in the future.

a. Corporate governance
b. Liability
c. False Claims Act
d. Vested

9. _________ are securities that can be easily converted into cash. Such securities will generally have highly liquid markets allowing the security to be sold at a reasonable price very quickly.This is a usual feature in real estate .

a. 3M Company
b. Tracking stock
c. BMC Software, Inc.
d. Marketable

10. _________ in economics and business is the result of an exchange and from that trade we assign a numerical monetary value to a good, service or asset. If Alice trades Bob 4 apples for an orange, the _________ of an orange is 4 apples. Inversely, the _________ of an apple is 1/4 oranges.

a. Discounts and allowances
b. Price discrimination
c. Transactional Net Margin Method
d. Price

11. A _________ is a fungible, negotiable instrument representing financial value. they are broadly categorized into debt securities (such as banknotes, bonds and debentures), and equity securities; e.g., common stocks. The company or other entity issuing the _________ is called the issuer.

a. 3M Company
b. BMC Software, Inc.
c. Tracking stock
d. Security

12. A _________ is any one of a variety of different systems, institutions, procedures, social relations and infrastructures whereby persons trade, and goods and services are exchanged, forming part of the economy. It is an arrangement that allows buyers and sellers to exchange things. _________s vary in size, range, geographic scale, location, types and variety of human communities, as well as the types of goods and services traded.

a. Recession
b. Market
c. Market Failure
d. Perfect competition

13. _________ is the price at which an asset would trade in a competitive Walrasian auction setting. _________ is often used interchangeably with open _________, fair value or fair _________, although these terms have distinct definitions in different standards, and may differ in some circumstances.

International Valuation Standards defines _________ as 'the estimated amount for which a property should exchange on the date of valuation between a willing buyer and a willing seller in an arme;s-length transaction after proper marketing wherein the parties had each acted knowledgeably, prudently, and without compulsion.'

_________ is a concept distinct from market price, which is e;the price at which one can transacte;, while _________ is e;the true underlying valuee; according to theoretical standards.

a. Sinking fund
b. Debtor
c. Market value
d. Segregated portfolio company

14. _________ is the term used to refer to the standard framework of guidelines for financial accounting used in any given jurisdiction. _________ includes the standards, conventions, and rules accountants follow in recording and summarizing transactions, and in the preparation of financial statements.

Financial accounting information must be assembled and reported objectively.

a. General ledger
b. Current asset
c. Long-term liabilities
d. Generally accepted accounting principles

15. _________ is generally understood in financial circles as the point at which revenue is recognized, typically through a transaction which involves the exchange of an asset, product, or service for cash or its equivalents.

This approach gives the accounting division a strictly objective basis for changing the books. For example, a homeowner may believe that his house has grown in value during a strong market, or fallen in value during a weak market, but until the house is actually sold for a specific price to a specific buyer, the change in value can only be estimated and is considered unrealized.

a. Valuation
b. Realization
c. Merck ' Co., Inc.
d. Total-factor productivity

16. A _________ is the pinnacle activity involved in selling products or services in return for money or other compensation. It is an act of completion of a commercial activity.

A _________ is completed by the seller, the owner of the goods.

a. High yield stock
b. Maturity
c. Sale
d. Tertiary sector of economy

17. _________ refers to a business or organization attempting to acquire goods or services to accomplish the goals of the enterprise. Though there are several organizations that attempt to set standards in the _________ process, processes can vary greatly between organizations. Typically the word e;_________e; is not used interchangeably with the word e;procuremente;, since procurement typically includes Expediting, Supplier Quality, and Traffic and Logistics (T'L) in addition to _________.

a. Consignor
b. Supply chain
c. Free port
d. Purchasing

18. _________ are payments made by a corporation to its shareholder members. It is the portion of corporate profits paid out to stockholders. When a corporation earns a profit or surplus, that money can be put to two uses: it can either be re-invested in the business (called retained earnings), or it can be paid to the shareholders as a dividend.

a. Dividends
b. Dividend payout ratio
c. Dividend yield
d. Dividend stripping

19. _________ in accounting is the process of treating equity investments, usually 20-50%, in associate companies. The investor keeps such equities as an asset. Proportional share of associate company's net income increases the investment, and proportional payment of dividends decreases it.

a. AIG
b. ABC Television Network
c. Out-of-pocket
d. Equity method

20. A mutual shareholder or _________ is an individual or company (including a corporation) that legally owns one or more shares of stock in a joint stock company. A company's shareholders collectively own that company. Thus, the typical goal of such companies is to enhance shareholder value.

a. 3M Company
b. Stock split
c. Growth investing
d. Stockholder

21. _________ in a corporation means to have control of a large enough block of voting stock shares in a company such that no one stock holder or coalition of stock holders can successfully oppose a motion. In theory this normally means that _________ would be 50% of the voting shares plus one.

In practice, though, _________ can be far less than that, as it is rare that 100% of a company's voting shareholders actively vote.

a. Participating preferred stock
b. Controlling interest
c. Public offering
d. Preferred stock

22. _________ is the state or fact of exclusive rights and control over property, which may be an object, land/real estate or intellectual property. An _________ right is also referred to as title.

_________ is the key building block in the development of the capitalist socio-economic system.

a. Encumbrance
b. ABC Television Network
c. Administrative proceeding
d. Ownership

23. A _________ is a company that owns enough voting stock in another firm to control management and operations by influencing or electing its board of directors; the second company being deemed as a subsidiary of the _________. The definition of a _________ differs from jurisdiction to jurisdiction, with the definition normally being defined by way of laws dealing with companies in that jurisdiction.

The _________-subsidiary company relationship is defined by Part 1.2, Division 6, Section 46 of the Corporations Act 2001 (Cth), which states:

A body corporate (in this section called the first body) is a subsidiary of another body corporate if, and only if:

(a) the other body:

(i) controls the composition of the first body's board; or

(ii) is in a position to cast, or control the casting of, more than one-half of the maximum number of votes that might be cast at a general meeting of the first body; or

(iii) holds more than one-half of the issued share capital of the first body (excluding any part of that issued share capital that carries no right to participate beyond a specified amount in a distribution of either profits or capital); or

(b) the first body is a subsidiary of a subsidiary of the other body.

a. Subsidiary
b. 3M Company
c. BMC Software, Inc.
d. Parent company

24. A _________, in business matters, is an entity that is controlled by a bigger and more powerful entity. The controlled entity is called a company, corporation, or limited liability company, and the controlling entity is called its parent (or the parent company.) The reason for this distinction is that a lone company cannot be a _________ of any organization; only an entity representing a legal fiction as a separate entity can be a _________.

a. Parent company
b. Subsidiary
c. BMC Software, Inc.
d. 3M Company

25. _________ is a fee paid on borrowed assets. It is the price paid for the use of borrowed money , or, money earned by deposited funds .Assets that are sometimes lent with _________ include money, shares, consumer goods through hire purchase, major assets such as aircraft, and even entire factories in finance lease arrangements. The _________ is calculated upon the value of the assets in the same manner as upon money.

a. ABC Television Network
b. Insolvency
c. AIG
d. Interest

26. _________ are formal records of a business' financial activities.

In British English, including United Kingdom company law, _________ are often referred to as accounts, although the term _________ is also used, particularly by accountants.

_________ provide an overview of a business' financial condition in both short and long term.

a. 3M Company
b. Notes to the financial statements
c. Statement of retained earnings
d. Financial statements

27. An _________ is a period with reference to which United Kingdom corporation tax is charged. It helps dictate when tax is paid on income and gains. An _________ begins whenever a company comes within the corporation tax charge, and whenever an _________ ends without the company ceasing to be within the charge.

a. AMEX
b. Accounting period
c. AIG
d. ABC Television Network

28. _________ are financial statements that factor the holding company's subsidiaries into its aggregated accounting figure. It is a representation of how the holding company is doing as a group. The consolidated accounts should provide a true and fair view of the financial and operating conditions of the group.

a. Committee on Accounting Procedure
b. Consolidated financial statements
c. Redemption value
d. Replacement cost

29. The _________ is a form of financial accounting system. The most common _________ is the petty cash system.

The _________ ensures that you must document how the petty cash is spent. In a petty cash system, petty cash dockets are written for each amount issued. So when all of these dockets are totalled at the end of the month and deducted from the opening petty cash float, the calculated value must agree with what is left in the petty cash float. Under the _________, only that which is recorded as spent is replenished.

a. ABC Television Network
b. AMEX
c. Imprest system
d. AIG

30. _________ in business is an accounting concept that refers to ownership of a company (subsidiary) that is less than 50% of outstanding shares. _________ belongs to other investors and is reported on the consolidated balance sheet of the owning company to reflect the claim on assets belonging to other, non-controlling shareholders. Also, _________ is reported on the consolidated income statement as a share of profit belonging to minority shareholders.

a. Minority interest
b. Credit memo
c. Bankruptcy prediction
d. Subledger

31. In economics, business, retail, and accounting, a _________ is the value of money that has been used up to produce something, and hence is not available for use anymore. In economics, a _________ is an alternative that is given up as a result of a decision. In business, the _________ may be one of acquisition, in which case the amount of money expended to acquire it is counted as _________.

a. Prime cost
b. Cost of quality
c. Cost allocation
d. Cost

32. _________ are sometimes the same as net worth, or shareholders' equity - assets minus liabilities. The term _________ is commonly used with charities or not for profit entities. Although these entities don't make money, it is important to maintain reasonable reserves to help future growth.

a. Sortino ratio
b. Debtor days
c. Net interest spread
d. Net assets

33. _________ is often a small amount of discretionary funds in the form of cash used for expenditures where it is not sensible to make the disbursement by check, because of the inconvenience and costs of writing, signing and then cashing the check.

The most common way of accounting expenditures is to use the imprest system. The initial fund would be created by issuing a check for the desired amount.

a. Remittance advice
b. Minority interest
c. Fixed asset
d. Petty cash

34. In finance, a _________ is a debt security, in which the authorized issuer owes the holders a debt and, depending on the terms of the _________, is obliged to pay interest (the coupon) and/or to repay the principal at a later date, termed maturity. It is a formal contract to repay borrowed money with interest at fixed intervals.

Thus a _________ is like a loan: the issuer is the borrower, the _________ holder is the lender, and the coupon is the interest.

a. Coupon rate
b. Zero-coupon bond
c. Revenue bonds
d. Bond

35. A _________, also referred to as a note payable in accounting, is a contract where one party (the maker or issuer) makes an unconditional promise in writing to pay a sum of money to the other (the payee), either at a fixed or determinable future time or on demand of the payee, under specific terms. They differ from IOUs in that they contain a specific promise to pay, rather than simply acknowledging that a debt exists.

The terms of a note typically include the principal amount, the interest rate if any, and the maturity date.

a. 3M Company
b. BMC Software, Inc.
c. Promissory note
d. BNSF Railway

36. A _________ is a type of bond that allows the issuer of the bond to retain the privilege of redeeming the bond at some point before the bond reaches the date of maturity. In other words, on the call dates, the issuer has the right, but not the obligation, to buy back the bonds from the bond holders at the call price. Technically speaking, the bonds are not really bought and held by the issuer but cancelled immediately.

a. Coupon rate
b. Catastrophe bonds
c. Callable bond
d. Zero-coupon

37. A loan is a type of debt. Like all debt instruments, a loan entails the redistribution of financial assets over time, between the _________ and the borrower.

In a loan, the borrower initially receives or borrows an amount of money, called the principal, from the _________, and is obligated to pay back or repay an equal amount of money to the _________ at a later time.

a. Credit rating
b. Lender
c. Debt
d. Loan to value

38. _________ is a life of security. It may also refer to the final payment date of a loan or other financial instrument, at which point all remaining interest and principal is due to be paid.

1, 3, 6 months _________ band can be calculated by using 30-day per month periods. For _________ bands over a year it is acceptable to use 365 day per year. For example with a Treasury Bond, its _________ is the date on which the principal is paid.

a. Statements of Financial Accounting Standards No. 133, Accounting for Derivative Instruments and Hedging Activities
b. Maturity
c. Factor
d. The Goodyear Tire ' Rubber Company

39. In finance, the _________ between two currencies specifies how much one currency is worth in terms of the other. It is the value of a foreign nation's currency in terms of the home nation's currency. For example an _________ of 102 Japanese yen to the United States dollar means that JPY 102 is worth the same as USD 1.
a. AMEX
b. Exchange rate
c. ABC Television Network
d. AIG

40. In monetary economics _________ can refer either to a particular _________, for example British Pounds or United States Dollars, or, to the coins and banknotes of a particular _________, which actually form only a small part of the monetary base of a nation's money supply. The other part of a nation's money supply consists of money deposited in banks (sometimes called deposit money), ownership of which can be transferred by means of checks (cheques in the United Kingdom and Australia) or other forms of money transfer such as credit and debit cards. Deposit money and _________ are 'money' in the sense that both are acceptable as a means of exchange, but money need not necessarily be '_________'.
a. Currency
b. 3M Company
c. BNSF Railway
d. BMC Software, Inc.

41. In United States banking, _________ is a marketing term for certain services offered primarily to larger business customers. It may be used to describe all bank accounts (such as checking accounts) provided to businesses of a certain size, but it is more often used to describe specific services such as cash concentration, zero balance accounting, and automated clearing house facilities. Sometimes, private banking customers are given _________ services.
a. 3M Company
b. Finance lease
c. Profitability index
d. Cash management

42. _________ is a company's financial statement that indicates how the revenue is transformed into the net income The purpose of the _________ is to show managers and investors whether the company made or lost money during the period being reported.

The important thing to remember about an _________ is that it represents a period of time.

a. ABC Television Network
b. Income statement
c. AMEX
d. AIG

43. In accounting, _________ has a very specific meaning. It is an outflow of cash or other valuable assets from a person or company to another person or company. This outflow of cash is generally one side of a trade for products or services that have equal or better current or future value to the buyer than to the seller.

a. ABC Television Network
b. AIG
c. AMEX
d. Expense

44. _________ is equal to the income that a firm has after subtracting costs and expenses from the total revenue. _________ can be distributed among holders of common stock as a dividend or held by the firm as retained earnings.

The items deducted will typically include tax expense, financing expense (interest expense), and minority interest. Likewise, preferred stock dividends will be subtracted too, though they are not an expense.

a. Long-term liabilities
b. Matching principle
c. Net income
d. Generally accepted accounting principles

45. The _________ is a private, not-for-profit organization whose primary purpose is to develop generally accepted accounting principles (GAAP) within the United States in the public's interest. The Securities and Exchange Commission (SEC) designated the _________ as the organization responsible for setting accounting standards for public companies in the U.S. It was created in 1973, replacing the Accounting Principles Board and the Committee on Accounting Procedure of the American Institute of Certified Public Accountants. The _________'s mission is 'to establish and improve standards of financial accounting and reporting for the guidance and education of the public, including issuers, auditors, and users of financial information.'

The _________ is not a governmental body.

a. Public company
b. Fannie Mae
c. Governmental Accounting Standards Board
d. Financial Accounting Standards Board

46. In financial accounting, a _________ or Statement of cash flows is a financial statement that shows a company's flow of cash. The money coming into the business is called cash inflow, and money going out from the business is called cash outflow. The statement shows how changes in balance sheet and income accounts affect cash and cash equivalents, and breaks the analysis down to operating, investing, and financing activities.

a. BMC Software, Inc.
b. Cash flow statement
c. BNSF Railway
d. 3M Company

47. A _________ is the transfer of wealth from one party (such as a person or company) to another. A _________ is usually made in exchange for the provision of goods, services or both, or to fulfill a legal obligation.

The simplest and oldest form of _________ is barter, the exchange of one good or service for another.

a. Payee
b. 3M Company
c. BMC Software, Inc.
d. Payment

1. _________ is a specific term used in companies' financial reporting from the company-whole point of view. Because that use excludes the effects of changing ownership interest, an economic measure of _________ is necessary for financial analysis from the shareholders' point of view

_________ is defined by the Financial Accounting Standards Board, or FASB, as 'the change in equity [net assets] of a business enterprise during a period from transactions and other events and circumstances from nonowner sources. It includes all changes in equity during a period except those resulting from investments by owners and distributions to owners.'

_________ is the sum of net income and other items that must bypass the income statement because they have not been realized, including items like an unrealized holding gain or loss from available for sale securities and foreign currency translation gains or losses.

a. Comprehensive income
b. BNSF Railway
c. 3M Company
d. BMC Software, Inc.

2. _________ is a company's financial statement that indicates how the revenue is transformed into the net income The purpose of the _________ is to show managers and investors whether the company made or lost money during the period being reported.

The important thing to remember about an _________ is that it represents a period of time.

a. ABC Television Network
b. AIG
c. AMEX
d. Income statement

3. _________ is equal to the income that a firm has after subtracting costs and expenses from the total revenue. _________ can be distributed among holders of common stock as a dividend or held by the firm as retained earnings.

The items deducted will typically include tax expense, financing expense (interest expense), and minority interest. Likewise, preferred stock dividends will be subtracted too, though they are not an expense.

a. Generally accepted accounting principles
b. Matching principle
c. Net income
d. Long-term liabilities

4. In accounting, _________ has a very specific meaning. It is an outflow of cash or other valuable assets from a person or company to another person or company. This outflow of cash is generally one side of a trade for products or services that have equal or better current or future value to the buyer than to the seller.

a. Expense
b. AMEX
c. ABC Television Network
d. AIG

5. In business and finance accounting, _________ is equal to the gross profit minus overheads minus interest payable plus/minus one off items for a given time period (usually: accounting period.)

A common synonym for '_________' when discussing financial statements (which include a balance sheet and an income statement) is the bottom line. This term results from the traditional appearance of an income statement which shows all allocated revenues and expenses over a specified time period with the resulting summation on the bottom line of the report.

a. Cost of goods sold
b. Treasury stock
c. Salvage value
d. Net profit

6. _________ is a measure of the ratio between the net operating income produced by an asset (usually real estate) and its capital cost (the original price paid to buy the asset) or alternatively its current market value. The rate is calculated in a simple fashion as follows:

$$\text{Capitalization Rate} = \frac{\text{annual net operating income}}{\text{cost (or value)}}$$

For example, if a building is purchased for $1,000,000 sale price and it produces $100,000 in positive net operating income (the amount left over after fixed costs and variable costs are subtracted from gross lease income) during one year, then:

- $100,000 / $1,000,000 = 0.10 = 10%

The asset's _________ is ten percent.

_________s are an indirect measure of how fast an investment will pay for itself. In the example above, the purchased building will be fully capitalized (pay for itself) after ten years (100% divided by 10%.)

a. BMC Software, Inc.
b. BNSF Railway
c. 3M Company
d. Capitalization rate

7. _________ is the value on a given date of a future payment or series of future payments, discounted to reflect the time value of money and other factors such as investment risk. _________ calculations are widely used in business and economics to provide a means to compare cash flows at different times on a meaningful 'like to like' basis.

The most commonly applied model of the time value of money is compound interest.

a. Net present value
b. 3M Company
c. Future value
d. Present value

8. _________ is a term used with respect to a retailed product, indicating that the product is in the end of its product lifetime and a vendor will no longer be marketing, selling, or promoting a particular product and may also be limiting or ending support for the product. In the specific case of product sales, the term end-of-sale (EOS) has also been used. The term lifetime, after the last production date, depends on the product and is related to a customer's expected product lifetime.

a. ABC Television Network
b. AMEX
c. AIG
d. End-of-life

9. _________ is the term used to refer to the standard framework of guidelines for financial accounting used in any given jurisdiction. _________ includes the standards, conventions, and rules accountants follow in recording and summarizing transactions, and in the preparation of financial statements.

Financial accounting information must be assembled and reported objectively.

a. General ledger
b. Current asset
c. Long-term liabilities
d. Generally accepted accounting principles

10. An _________ is a term used in behavioral economics to describe those types of behaviors that impose costs on a person in the long-run that are not taken into account when making decisions in the present. Classical Economics discourages government from creating legislation that targets internalities, because it is assumed that the consumer takes these personal costs into account when paying for the good that causes the _________. For example, cigarettes should be taxed because of the negative consumption externalities that they impose, such as second-hand smoke, not because the smoker harms him or herself by smoking.

a. Internality
b. Authorised capital
c. Operating budget
d. Inventory turnover ratio

11. In accounting and organizational theory, _________ is defined as a process effected by an organization's structure, work and authority flows, people and management information systems, designed to help the organization accomplish specific goals or objectives. It is a means by which an organization's resources are directed, monitored, and measured. It plays an important role in preventing and detecting fraud and protecting the organization's resources, both physical (e.g., machinery and property) and intangible (e.g., reputation or intellectual property such as trademarks.)

a. Audit risk
b. Auditor independence
c. Audit committee
d. Internal control

12. _________ is a form of corporation equity ownership represented in the securities. It is a stock whose dividends are based on market fluctuations. It is dangerous in comparison to preferred shares and some other investment options, in that in the event of bankruptcy, _________ investors receive their funds after preferred stock holders, bondholders, creditors, etc. On the other hand, common shares on average perform better than preferred shares or bonds over time.

a. Common stock
b. 3M Company
c. Stock split
d. Growth investing

13. _________ are payments made by a corporation to its shareholder members. It is the portion of corporate profits paid out to stockholders. When a corporation earns a profit or surplus, that money can be put to two uses: it can either be re-invested in the business (called retained earnings), or it can be paid to the shareholders as a dividend.

a. Dividend yield
b. Dividend payout ratio
c. Dividend stripping
d. Dividends

14. _________ are the earnings returned on the initial investment amount.

In the US, the Financial Accounting Standards Board (FASB) requires companies' income statements to report _________ for each of the major categories of the income statement: continuing operations, discontinued operations, extraordinary items, and net income.

The _________ formula does not include preferred dividends for categories outside of continued operations and net income.

a. Average accounting return
b. Earnings yield
c. Invested capital
d. Earnings per share

15. _________ is typically a 'higher ranking' stock than voting shares, and its terms are negotiated between the corporation and the investor.

_________ usually carries no voting rights, but may carry superior priority over common stock in the payment of dividends and upon liquidation. _________ may carry a dividend that is paid out prior to any dividends being paid to common stock holders.

a. Gross income
b. Cash flow
c. Restricted stock
d. Preferred stock

16. In business and accounting, _________ are everything of value that is owned by a person or company. It is a claim on the property your income of a borrower. The balance sheet of a firm records the monetary value of the _________ owned by the firm.

a. Accounts receivable
b. Earnings before interest, taxes, depreciation and amortization
c. Accrual basis accounting
d. Assets

17. In accounting, _________ or carrying value is the value of an asset according to its balance sheet account balance. For assets, the value is based on the original cost of the asset less any depreciation, amortization or impairment costs made against the asset. Traditionally, a company's _________ is its total assets minus intangible assets and liabilities.

a. Generally accepted accounting principles
b. Matching principle
c. Book value
d. Depreciation

18. _________ is the state or fact of exclusive rights and control over property, which may be an object, land/real estate or intellectual property. An _________ right is also referred to as title.

_________ is the key building block in the development of the capitalist socio-economic system.

a. Administrative proceeding
b. ABC Television Network
c. Ownership
d. Encumbrance

19. A mutual shareholder or _________ is an individual or company (including a corporation) that legally owns one or more shares of stock in a joint stock company. A company's shareholders collectively own that company. Thus, the typical goal of such companies is to enhance shareholder value.

a. Stock split
b. Growth investing
c. Stockholder
d. 3M Company

20. _________ is the balance of the amounts of cash being received and paid by a business during a defined period of time, sometimes tied to a specific project. Measurement of _________ can be used

- to evaluate the state or performance of a business or project.
- to determine problems with liquidity. Being profitable does not necessarily mean being liquid. A company can fail because of a shortage of cash, even while profitable.
- to project rate of returns. The time of _________s into and out of projects are used as inputs to financial models such as internal rate of return, and net present value.
- to examine income or growth of a business when it is believed that accrual accounting concepts do not represent economic realities. Alternately, _________ can be used to 'validate' the net income generated by accrual accounting.

_________ as a generic term may be used differently depending on context, and certain _________ definitions may be adapted by analysts and users for their own uses. Common terms include operating _________ and free _________.

a. Cash flow
b. Flow-through entity
c. Controlling interest
d. Commercial paper

21. The _________ is a form of financial accounting system. The most common _________ is the petty cash system.

The _________ ensures that you must document how the petty cash is spent. In a petty cash system, petty cash dockets are written for each amount issued. So when all of these dockets are totalled at the end of the month and deducted from the opening petty cash float, the calculated value must agree with what is left in the petty cash float. Under the _________, only that which is recorded as spent is replenished.

a. Imprest system
b. AIG
c. AMEX
d. ABC Television Network

22. In financial accounting, a _________ or Statement of cash flows is a financial statement that shows a company's flow of cash. The money coming into the business is called cash inflow, and money going out from the business is called cash outflow. The statement shows how changes in balance sheet and income accounts affect cash and cash equivalents, and breaks the analysis down to operating, investing, and financing activities.

a. BNSF Railway
b. 3M Company
c. BMC Software, Inc.
d. Cash flow statement

23. A _________ is the transfer of wealth from one party (such as a person or company) to another. A _________ is usually made in exchange for the provision of goods, services or both, or to fulfill a legal obligation.

The simplest and oldest form of _________ is barter, the exchange of one good or service for another.

a. Payee
b. 3M Company
c. BMC Software, Inc.
d. Payment

24. _________ is often a small amount of discretionary funds in the form of cash used for expenditures where it is not sensible to make the disbursement by check, because of the inconvenience and costs of writing, signing and then cashing the check.

The most common way of accounting expenditures is to use the imprest system. The initial fund would be created by issuing a check for the desired amount.

a. Fixed asset
b. Minority interest
c. Remittance advice
d. Petty cash

25. An _________ is a tax levied on the financial income of people, corporations, or other legal entities. Various _________ systems exist, with varying degrees of tax incidence. Income taxation can be progressive, proportional, or regressive.

a. Implied level of government service
b. Individual Retirement Arrangement
c. Ordinary income
d. Income tax

26. _________ methods are means of managing inventory and financial matters involving the money a company ties up within inventory of produced goods, raw materials, parts, components, or feed stocks. FIFO stands for first-in, first-out, meaning that the oldest inventory items are recorded as sold first. LIFO stands for last-in, first-out, meaning that the most recently purchased items are recorded as sold first.

a. Reorder point
b. 3M Company
c. Finished good
d. FIFO and LIFO accounting

27. U.S. _________ refers to accounting for tax purposes in the United States. Unlike most countries, the United States has a comprehensive set of accounting principles for tax purposes, prescribed by tax law, which are separate and distinct from Generally Accepted Accounting Principles.

The Internal Revenue Code governs the application of _________.

a. BNSF Railway
b. 3M Company
c. Tax accounting
d. BMC Software, Inc.

28. _________ is the portion of income that is the subject of taxation according to the laws that determine what is income and the taxation rate for that income. Generally, _________ refers to an individual's (or corporation's) gross income, adjusted for various deductions allowable by statute. The main questions put by most individuals in any jurisdiction are 'what makes up my _________' and what tax rates should be applied such that I can work out my tax liability to the state.

a. SUTA dumping
b. Taxable income
c. Reverse Morris trust
d. Half-year convention

29. _________, in accrual accounting, is any account where the asset or liability is not realized until a future date (accounting period), e.g. annuities, charges, taxes, income, etc. The _________ item may be carried, dependent on type of deferral, as either an asset or liability.

a. Pro forma
b. Deferred
c. Cash basis accounting
d. Payroll

30. In financial accounting, a _________ is defined as an obligation of an entity arising from past transactions or events, the settlement of which may result in the transfer or use of assets, provision of services or other yielding of economic benefits in the future.

a. Corporate governance
b. Liability
c. Vested
d. False Claims Act

31. In financial accounting, a _________ or statement of financial position is a summary of a person's or organization's balances. Assets, liabilities and ownership equity are listed as of a specific date, such as the end of its financial year. A _________ is often described as a snapshot of a company's financial condition.

a. Financial statements
b. Balance sheet
c. 3M Company
d. Statement of retained earnings

32. The _________ is one of the basic financial statements as per Generally Accepted Accounting Principles, and it explains the changes in a company's retained earnings over the reporting period. It breaks down changes affecting the account, such as profits or losses from operations, dividends paid, and any other items charged or credited to retained earnings. A retained earnings statement is required by Generally Accepted Accounting Principles whenever comparative balance sheets and income statements are presented.

a. Statement of retained earnings
b. Notes to the financial statements
c. 3M Company
d. Financial statements

33. _________ is a fee paid on borrowed assets. It is the price paid for the use of borrowed money , or, money earned by deposited funds .Assets that are sometimes lent with _________ include money, shares, consumer goods through hire purchase, major assets such as aircraft, and even entire factories in finance lease arrangements. The _________ is calculated upon the value of the assets in the same manner as upon money.

a. ABC Television Network
b. Insolvency
c. AIG
d. Interest

34. _________ are formal records of a business' financial activities.

In British English, including United Kingdom company law, _________ are often referred to as accounts, although the term _________ is also used, particularly by accountants.

_________ provide an overview of a business' financial condition in both short and long term.

a. Notes to the financial statements
b. Financial statements
c. 3M Company
d. Statement of retained earnings

35. A _________ is a fungible, negotiable instrument representing financial value. they are broadly categorized into debt securities (such as banknotes, bonds and debentures), and equity securities; e.g., common stocks. The company or other entity issuing the _________ is called the issuer.

a. Security
b. BMC Software, Inc.
c. Tracking stock
d. 3M Company

36. The _________ of 1934 is a law governing the secondary trading of securities (stocks, bonds, and debentures) in the United States of America. The Act, 48 Stat. 881 (enacted June 6, 1934), codified at 15 U.S.C.

a. BNSF Railway
b. BMC Software, Inc.
c. Securities Exchange Act
d. 3M Company

37. The U.S. _________ is an independent agency of the United States government which holds primary responsibility for enforcing the federal securities laws and regulating the securities industry, the nation's stock and options exchanges, and other electronic securities markets. The SEC was created by section 4 of the Securities Exchange Act of 1934 (now codified as 15 U.S.C. ÂÂ§ 78d and commonly referred to as the 1934 Act.)

a. BNSF Railway
b. 3M Company
c. Securities and Exchange Commission
d. BMC Software, Inc.

38. An _________ is a period with reference to which United Kingdom corporation tax is charged. It helps dictate when tax is paid on income and gains. An _________ begins whenever a company comes within the corporation tax charge, and whenever an _________ ends without the company ceasing to be within the charge.

a. AIG
b. Accounting period
c. ABC Television Network
d. AMEX

39. The most frequent type of report is referred to as the Unqualified Opinion, and is regarded by many as the equivalent of a 'clean bill of health' to a patient, which has led many to call it the _________, but in reality it is not a clean bill of health. This type of report is issued by an auditor when the financial statements presented are free of material misstatements and are in accordance with GAAP, which in other words means that the company's financial condition, position, and operations are fairly presented in the financial statements. It is the best type of report an auditee may receive from an external auditor.

a. Financial Instruments and Exchange Law
b. Sales Tax Audit
c. Management assertions
d. Clean opinion

40. The general definition of an _________ is an evaluation of a person, organization, system, process, project or product. _________s are performed to ascertain the validity and reliability of information; also to provide an assessment of a system's internal control. The goal of an _________ is to express an opinion on the person/organization/system (etc) in question, under evaluation based on work done on a test basis.

a. Audit
b. Institute of Chartered Accountants of India
c. Assurance service
d. Audit regime

1. _________ is the balance of the amounts of cash being received and paid by a business during a defined period of time, sometimes tied to a specific project. Measurement of _________ can be used

- to evaluate the state or performance of a business or project.
- to determine problems with liquidity. Being profitable does not necessarily mean being liquid. A company can fail because of a shortage of cash, even while profitable.
- to project rate of returns. The time of _________s into and out of projects are used as inputs to financial models such as internal rate of return, and net present value.
- to examine income or growth of a business when it is believed that accrual accounting concepts do not represent economic realities. Alternately, _________ can be used to 'validate' the net income generated by accrual accounting.

_________ as a generic term may be used differently depending on context, and certain _________ definitions may be adapted by analysts and users for their own uses. Common terms include operating _________ and free _________.

a. Flow-through entity
b. Cash flow
c. Controlling interest
d. Commercial paper

2. _________ are formal records of a business' financial activities.

In British English, including United Kingdom company law, _________ are often referred to as accounts, although the term _________ is also used, particularly by accountants.

_________ provide an overview of a business' financial condition in both short and long term.

a. Financial statements
b. Notes to the financial statements
c. 3M Company
d. Statement of retained earnings

3. In financial accounting, a _________ or Statement of cash flows is a financial statement that shows a company's flow of cash. The money coming into the business is called cash inflow, and money going out from the business is called cash outflow. The statement shows how changes in balance sheet and income accounts affect cash and cash equivalents, and breaks the analysis down to operating, investing, and financing activities.

a. BNSF Railway
b. Cash flow statement
c. BMC Software, Inc.
d. 3M Company

4. In physics, and more specifically kinematics, _________ is the change in velocity over time. Because velocity is a vector, it can change in two ways: a change in magnitude and/or a change in direction. In one dimension, _________ is the rate at which something speeds up or slows down.

a. AMEX
b. AIG
c. ABC Television Network
d. Acceleration

5. _________ refers to any one of several methods by which a company, for 'financial accounting' and/or tax purposes, depreciates a fixed asset in such a way that the amount of depreciation taken each year is higher during the earlier years of an assete;s life. For financial accounting purposes, _________ is generally used when an asset is expected to be much more productive during its early years, so that depreciation expense will more accurately represent how much of an assete;s usefulness is being used up each year. For tax purposes, _________ provides a way of deferring corporate income taxes by reducing taxable income in current years, in exchange for increased taxable income in future years.

a. Indirect tax
b. Effective marginal tax rates
c. User charge
d. Accelerated depreciation

6. An _________ is a period with reference to which United Kingdom corporation tax is charged. It helps dictate when tax is paid on income and gains. An _________ begins whenever a company comes within the corporation tax charge, and whenever an _________ ends without the company ceasing to be within the charge.

a. ABC Television Network
b. AIG
c. AMEX
d. Accounting period

7. _________ is a term used in accounting, economics and finance to spread the cost of an asset over the span of several years.

In simple words we can say that _________ is the reduction in the value of an asset due to usage, passage of time, wear and tear, technological outdating or obsolescence, depletion, inadequacy, rot, rust, decay or other such factors.

In accounting, _________ is a term used to describe any method of attributing the historical or purchase cost of an asset across its useful life, roughly corresponding to normal wear and tear.

a. General ledger
b. Current asset
c. Depreciation
d. Net profit

8. A _________ is the transfer of wealth from one party (such as a person or company) to another. A _________ is usually made in exchange for the provision of goods, services or both, or to fulfill a legal obligation.

The simplest and oldest form of _________ is barter, the exchange of one good or service for another.

a. Payment
b. 3M Company
c. Payee
d. BMC Software, Inc.

9. _________ are the most liquid assets found within the asset portion of a company's balance sheet. Cash equivalents are assets that are readily convertible into cash, such as money market holdings, short-term government bonds or Treasury bills, marketable securities and commercial paper. _________ are distinguished from other investments through their short-term existence; they mature within 3 months whereas short-term investments are 12 months or less, and long-term investments are any investments that mature in excess of 12 months.

a. Cash and cash equivalents
b. Payback period
c. Par value
d. Debtor

10. _________ are payments made by a corporation to its shareholder members. It is the portion of corporate profits paid out to stockholders. When a corporation earns a profit or surplus, that money can be put to two uses: it can either be re-invested in the business (called retained earnings), or it can be paid to the shareholders as a dividend.

a. Dividends
b. Dividend stripping
c. Dividend payout ratio
d. Dividend yield

11. _________ is a specific term used in companies' financial reporting from the company-whole point of view. Because that use excludes the effects of changing ownership interest, an economic measure of _________ is necessary for financial analysis from the shareholders' point of view

_________ is defined by the Financial Accounting Standards Board, or FASB, as 'the change in equity [net assets] of a business enterprise during a period from transactions and other events and circumstances from nonowner sources. It includes all changes in equity during a period except those resulting from investments by owners and distributions to owners.'

_________ is the sum of net income and other items that must bypass the income statement because they have not been realized, including items like an unrealized holding gain or loss from available for sale securities and foreign currency translation gains or losses.

a. BNSF Railway
b. 3M Company
c. Comprehensive income
d. BMC Software, Inc.

12. _________ is equal to the income that a firm has after subtracting costs and expenses from the total revenue. _________ can be distributed among holders of common stock as a dividend or held by the firm as retained earnings.

The items deducted will typically include tax expense, financing expense (interest expense), and minority interest. Likewise, preferred stock dividends will be subtracted too, though they are not an expense.

a. Generally accepted accounting principles
b. Net income
c. Long-term liabilities
d. Matching principle

13. In accounting, _________ has a very specific meaning. It is an outflow of cash or other valuable assets from a person or company to another person or company. This outflow of cash is generally one side of a trade for products or services that have equal or better current or future value to the buyer than to the seller.

a. ABC Television Network
b. AIG
c. AMEX
d. Expense

14. In business and finance accounting, _________ is equal to the gross profit minus overheads minus interest payable plus/minus one off items for a given time period (usually: accounting period.)

A common synonym for '_________' when discussing financial statements (which include a balance sheet and an income statement) is the bottom line. This term results from the traditional appearance of an income statement which shows all allocated revenues and expenses over a specified time period with the resulting summation on the bottom line of the report.

a. Salvage value
b. Cost of goods sold
c. Treasury stock
d. Net profit

15. In economics, the concept of the _________ refers to the decision-making time frame of a firm in which at least one factor of production is fixed. Costs which are fixed in the _________ have no impact on a firms decisions. For example a firm can raise output by increasing the amount of labour through overtime.

a. 3M Company
b. Long-run
c. BMC Software, Inc.
d. Short-run

16. A mutual shareholder or _________ is an individual or company (including a corporation) that legally owns one or more shares of stock in a joint stock company. A company's shareholders collectively own that company. Thus, the typical goal of such companies is to enhance shareholder value.

a. Stockholder
b. 3M Company
c. Stock split
d. Growth investing

17. In financial accounting, a _________ or statement of financial position is a summary of a person's or organization's balances. Assets, liabilities and ownership equity are listed as of a specific date, such as the end of its financial year. A _________ is often described as a snapshot of a company's financial condition.

a. 3M Company
b. Balance sheet
c. Statement of retained earnings
d. Financial statements

18. In business and accounting, _________ are everything of value that is owned by a person or company. It is a claim on the property your income of a borrower. The balance sheet of a firm records the monetary value of the _________ owned by the firm.

a. Earnings before interest, taxes, depreciation and amortization
b. Accounts receivable
c. Accrual basis accounting
d. Assets

19. A _________ is a party (e.g. person, organization, company, or government) that has a claim to the services of a second party. It is a person or institution to whom money is owed. The first party, in general, has provided some property or service to the second party under the assumption (usually enforced by contract) that the second party will return an equivalent property or service.

a. Creditor
b. Treasury company
c. Payback period
d. Par value

20. _________ is a company's financial statement that indicates how the revenue is transformed into the net income The purpose of the _________ is to show managers and investors whether the company made or lost money during the period being reported.

The important thing to remember about an _________ is that it represents a period of time.

a. ABC Television Network
b. AIG
c. AMEX
d. Income statement

21. In financial accounting, a _________ is defined as an obligation of an entity arising from past transactions or events, the settlement of which may result in the transfer or use of assets, provision of services or other yielding of economic benefits in the future.

a. Corporate governance
b. False Claims Act
c. Vested
d. Liability

22. In economic models, the _________ time frame assumes no fixed factors of production. Firms can enter or leave the marketplace, and the cost (and availability) of land, labor, raw materials, and capital goods can be assumed to vary. In contrast, in the short-run time frame, certain factors are assumed to be fixed, because there is not sufficient time for them to change.

a. BMC Software, Inc.
b. Short-run
c. Long-run
d. 3M Company

23. Employment is a contract between two parties, one being the employer and the other being the _________. An _________ may be defined as: 'A person in the service of another under any contract of hire, express or implied, oral or written, where the employer has the power or right to control and direct the _________ in the material details of how the work is to be performed.' Black's Law Dictionary page 471 (5th ed. 1979.)

a. AIG
b. AMEX
c. ABC Television Network
d. Employee

24. An _________ is a tax levied on the financial income of people, corporations, or other legal entities. Various _________ systems exist, with varying degrees of tax incidence. Income taxation can be progressive, proportional, or regressive.

a. Individual Retirement Arrangement
b. Ordinary income
c. Income tax
d. Implied level of government service

25. _________ is a fee paid on borrowed assets. It is the price paid for the use of borrowed money , or, money earned by deposited funds .Assets that are sometimes lent with _________ include money, shares, consumer goods through hire purchase, major assets such as aircraft, and even entire factories in finance lease arrangements. The _________ is calculated upon the value of the assets in the same manner as upon money.

a. ABC Television Network
b. Insolvency
c. AIG
d. Interest

26. In financial accounting, _________ , cash flow provided by operations or cash flow from operating activities, refers to the amount of cash a company generates from the revenues it brings in, excluding costs associated with long-term investment on capital items or investment in securities.

_________ = Cash generated from operations less taxation and interest paid, investment income received and less dividends paid gives rise to _________s per International Financial Reporting Standards.

To calculate cash generated from operations, one must calculate cash generated from customers and cash paid to suppliers.

a. AMEX
b. ABC Television Network
c. Operating cash flow
d. AIG

27. _________ is the process of increasing, or accounting for, an amount over a period of time. Particular instances of the term include:

- _________, the allocation of a lump sum amount to different time periods, particularly for loans and other forms of finance, including related interest or other finance charges.
    - _________ schedule, a table detailing each periodic payment on a loan (typically a mortgage), as generated by an _________ calculator.
    - Negative _________, an _________ schedule where the loan amount actually increases through not paying the full interest
- Amortized analysis, analyzing the execution cost of algorithms over a sequence of operations.
- _________ of capital expenditures of certain assets under accounting rules, particularly intangible assets, in a manner analogous to depreciation.
- _________

a. Annuity
b. Intangible
c. EBIT
d. Amortization

28. In economics, business, retail, and accounting, a _________ is the value of money that has been used up to produce something, and hence is not available for use anymore. In economics, a _________ is an alternative that is given up as a result of a decision. In business, the _________ may be one of acquisition, in which case the amount of money expended to acquire it is counted as _________.

a. Cost allocation
b. Prime cost
c. Cost of quality
d. Cost

29. In accounting, a _________ is an asset on the balance sheet which is expected to be sold or otherwise used up in the near future, usually within one year, or one business cycle - whichever is longer. Typical _________s include cash, cash equivalents, accounts receivable, inventory, the portion of prepaid accounts which will be used within a year, and short-term investments.

On the balance sheet, assets will typically be classified into _________s and long-term assets.

a. Pro forma
b. Current asset
c. Deferred
d. General ledger

30. _________ is the term used to refer to the standard framework of guidelines for financial accounting used in any given jurisdiction. _________ includes the standards, conventions, and rules accountants follow in recording and summarizing transactions, and in the preparation of financial statements.

Financial accounting information must be assembled and reported objectively.

a. Long-term liabilities
b. Current asset
c. General ledger
d. Generally accepted accounting principles

31. A _________ is the pinnacle activity involved in selling products or services in return for money or other compensation. It is an act of completion of a commercial activity.

A _________ is completed by the seller, the owner of the goods.

a. Maturity
b. High yield stock
c. Sale
d. Tertiary sector of economy

32. _________ is any physical or virtual entity that is owned by an individual or jointly by a group of individuals. An owner of _________ has the right to consume, sell, rent, mortgage, transfer and exchange his or her _________. Important widely-recognized types of _________ include real _________, personal _________ (other physical possessions), and intellectual _________ (rights over artistic creations, inventions, etc.), although the latter is not always as widely recognized or enforced.

a. Disclosure requirement
b. Fiduciary
c. Property
d. Primary authority

33. _________, also known as property, plant, and equipment (PP&E), is a term used in accountancy for assets and property which cannot easily be converted into cash. This can be compared with current assets such as cash or bank accounts, which are described as liquid assets. In most cases, only tangible assets are referred to as fixed.

a. Minority interest
b. Bankruptcy prediction
c. Subledger
d. Fixed asset

34. _________ is a form of corporation equity ownership represented in the securities. It is a stock whose dividends are based on market fluctuations. It is dangerous in comparison to preferred shares and some other investment options, in that in the event of bankruptcy, _________ investors receive their funds after preferred stock holders, bondholders, creditors, etc. On the other hand, common shares on average perform better than preferred shares or bonds over time.

a. 3M Company
b. Growth investing
c. Stock split
d. Common stock

35. _________ is typically a 'higher ranking' stock than voting shares, and its terms are negotiated between the corporation and the investor.

_________ usually carries no voting rights, but may carry superior priority over common stock in the payment of dividends and upon liquidation. _________ may carry a dividend that is paid out prior to any dividends being paid to common stock holders.

a. Gross income
b. Restricted stock
c. Cash flow
d. Preferred stock

36. A _________ or reacquired stock is stock which is bought back by the issuing company, reducing the amount of outstanding stock on the open market ('open market' including insiders' holdings).

Stock repurchases are often used as a tax-efficient method to put cash into shareholders' hands, rather than pay dividends. Sometimes, companies do this when they feel that their stock is undervalued on the open market.

a. Net profit
b. Cost of goods sold
c. Matching principle
d. Treasury stock

37. _________ is that which is owed; usually referencing assets owed, but the term can also cover moral obligations and other interactions not requiring money. In the case of assets, _________ is a means of using future purchasing power in the present before a summation has been earned. Some companies and corporations use _________ as a part of their overall corporate finance strategy.

a. Lender
b. Loan
c. Debenture
d. Debt

38. _________ relates to the cost of borrowing money. It is the price that a lender charges a borrower for the use of the lender's money. _________ is different from OPEX and CAPEX, for it relates to the capital structure of a company.

a. Interest
b. Interest expense
c. AIG
d. ABC Television Network

39. In finance, a _________ is a debt security, in which the authorized issuer owes the holders a debt and, depending on the terms of the _________, is obliged to pay interest (the coupon) and/or to repay the principal at a later date, termed maturity. It is a formal contract to repay borrowed money with interest at fixed intervals.

Thus a _________ is like a loan: the issuer is the borrower, the _________ holder is the lender, and the coupon is the interest.

a. Zero-coupon bond
b. Coupon rate
c. Revenue bonds
d. Bond

40. In finance, a _________ is the party in a loan agreement which receives money or other instrument from a lender and promises to repay the lender in a specified time.

a. Simple interest
b. BMC Software, Inc.
c. 3M Company
d. Borrower

41. A loan is a type of debt. Like all debt instruments, a loan entails the redistribution of financial assets over time, between the _________ and the borrower.

In a loan, the borrower initially receives or borrows an amount of money, called the principal, from the _________, and is obligated to pay back or repay an equal amount of money to the _________ at a later time.

a. Loan to value
b. Debt
c. Credit rating
d. Lender

42. At its simplest, a company's _________ as it sometimes called, is computed in by multiplying the income before tax number, as reported to shareholders, by the appropriate tax rate. In reality, the computation is typically considerably more complex due to things such as expenses considered not deductible by taxing authorities ('add backs'), the range of tax rates applicable to various levels of income, different tax rates in different jurisdictions, multiple layers of tax on income, and other issues.

Historically, in many places, a revenue-expense method was used, in which the income statement was seen as primary, and the balance sheet as secondary.

a. 3M Company
b. Payroll
c. Total Expense Ratio
d. Tax expense

43. A _________, also client, buyer or purchaser is the buyer or user of the paid products of an individual or organization, mostly called the supplier or seller. This is typically through purchasing or renting goods or services.

a. BNSF Railway
b. BMC Software, Inc.
c. 3M Company
d. Customer

44. An _________, operating expenditure, operational expense, operational expenditure or OPEX is an on-going cost for running a product, business, or system. Its counterpart, a capital expenditure (CAPEX), is the cost of developing or providing non-consumable parts for the product or system. For example, the purchase of a photocopier is the CAPEX, and the annual paper and toner cost is the OPEX.

a. ABC Television Network
b. AIG
c. Operating expense
d. AMEX

45. In corporate finance, _________ is a cash flow available for distribution among all the security holders of a company. They include equity holders, debt holders, preferred stock holders, convertible security holders, and so on.

a. Free cash flow
b. Tax profit
c. Procurement
d. Product life cycle

1. _________ are formal records of a business' financial activities.

In British English, including United Kingdom company law, _________ are often referred to as accounts, although the term _________ is also used, particularly by accountants.

_________ provide an overview of a business' financial condition in both short and long term.

a. Financial statements
b. Statement of retained earnings
c. 3M Company
d. Notes to the financial statements

2. An _________ is a period with reference to which United Kingdom corporation tax is charged. It helps dictate when tax is paid on income and gains. An _________ begins whenever a company comes within the corporation tax charge, and whenever an _________ ends without the company ceasing to be within the charge.

a. AMEX
b. Accounting period
c. ABC Television Network
d. AIG

3. In financial accounting, a _________ or statement of financial position is a summary of a person's or organization's balances. Assets, liabilities and ownership equity are listed as of a specific date, such as the end of its financial year. A _________ is often described as a snapshot of a company's financial condition.

a. Statement of retained earnings
b. 3M Company
c. Financial statements
d. Balance sheet

4. _________ is a company's financial statement that indicates how the revenue is transformed into the net income The purpose of the _________ is to show managers and investors whether the company made or lost money during the period being reported.

The important thing to remember about an _________ is that it represents a period of time.

a. AMEX
b. ABC Television Network
c. AIG
d. Income statement

5. In business and accounting, _________ are everything of value that is owned by a person or company. It is a claim on the property your income of a borrower. The balance sheet of a firm records the monetary value of the _________ owned by the firm.

a. Earnings before interest, taxes, depreciation and amortization
b. Accrual basis accounting
c. Accounts receivable
d. Assets

6. _________ is the balance of the amounts of cash being received and paid by a business during a defined period of time, sometimes tied to a specific project. Measurement of _________ can be used

- to evaluate the state or performance of a business or project.
- to determine problems with liquidity. Being profitable does not necessarily mean being liquid. A company can fail because of a shortage of cash, even while profitable.
- to project rate of returns. The time of _________s into and out of projects are used as inputs to financial models such as internal rate of return, and net present value.
- to examine income or growth of a business when it is believed that accrual accounting concepts do not represent economic realities. Alternately, _________ can be used to 'validate' the net income generated by accrual accounting.

_________ as a generic term may be used differently depending on context, and certain _________ definitions may be adapted by analysts and users for their own uses. Common terms include operating _________ and free _________.

a. Controlling interest
b. Commercial paper
c. Flow-through entity
d. Cash flow

7. In accounting, _________ has a very specific meaning. It is an outflow of cash or other valuable assets from a person or company to another person or company. This outflow of cash is generally one side of a trade for products or services that have equal or better current or future value to the buyer than to the seller.

a. AMEX
b. ABC Television Network
c. AIG
d. Expense

8. In financial accounting, a _________ is defined as an obligation of an entity arising from past transactions or events, the settlement of which may result in the transfer or use of assets, provision of services or other yielding of economic benefits in the future.

a. False Claims Act
b. Vested
c. Corporate governance
d. Liability

9. _________ is equal to the income that a firm has after subtracting costs and expenses from the total revenue. _________ can be distributed among holders of common stock as a dividend or held by the firm as retained earnings.

The items deducted will typically include tax expense, financing expense (interest expense), and minority interest. Likewise, preferred stock dividends will be subtracted too, though they are not an expense.

a. Net income
b. Long-term liabilities
c. Matching principle
d. Generally accepted accounting principles

10. The term '_________' refers to the concept of collecting information and attempting to spot a pattern in the information. In some fields of study, the term '_________' has more formally-defined meanings.

In project management _________ is a mathematical technique that uses historical results to predict future outcome.

a. Trend analysis
b. Regression analysis
c. 3M Company
d. Multicollinearity

11. _________ is an organization's process of defining its strategy and making decisions on allocating its resources to pursue this strategy, including its capital and people. Various business analysis techniques can be used in _________, including SWOT analysis (Strengths, Weaknesses, Opportunities, and Threats) and PEST analysis (Political, Economic, Social, and Technological analysis) or STEER analysis involving Socio-cultural, Technological, Economic, Ecological, and Regulatory factors and EPISTEL (Environment, Political, Informatic, Social, Technological, Economic and Legal)

_________ is the formal consideration of an organization's future course. All _________ deals with at least one of three key questions:

1. 'What do we do?'
2. 'For whom do we do it?'
3. 'How do we excel?'

In business _________, the third question is better phrased 'How can we beat or avoid competition?'. (Bradford and Duncan, page 1.)

a. BNSF Railway
b. BMC Software, Inc.
c. 3M Company
d. Strategic planning

12. In economics, _________ or _________ goods or real _________ refers to factors of production used to create goods or services that are not themselves significantly consumed (though they may depreciate) in the production process. _________ goods may be acquired with money or financial _________. In finance and accounting, _________ generally refers to financial wealth, especially that used to start or maintain a business.

a. Disclosure
b. Screening
c. Vyborg Appeal
d. Capital

13. _________ is a type of lease - the other being an operating lease. A _________ effectively allows a firm to finance the purchase of an asset, even if, strictly speaking, the firm never acquires the asset. Typically, a _________ will give the lessee control over an asset for a large proportion of the asset's useful life, providing them the benefits and risks of ownership.

a. Profitability index
b. Finance lease
c. 3M Company
d. Debt ratio

14. A _________ is a contract conferring a right on one person to possess property belonging to another person (called a landlord or lessor) to the exclusion of the owner landlord. It is a rental agreement between landlord and tenant. The relationship between the tenant and the landlord is called a tenancy, and the right to possession by the tenant is sometimes called a leasehold interest.

a. Robinson-Patman Act
b. Lease
c. Model Code of Professional Responsibility
d. Federal Sentencing Guidelines

15. _________ is the process of comparing the cost, cycle time, productivity, or quality of a specific process or method to another that is widely considered to be an industry standard or best practice. Essentially, _________ provides a snapshot of the performance of your business and helps you understand where you are in relation to a particular standard. The result is often a business case for making changes in order to make improvements.

a. 3M Company
b. Strategic business unit
c. Benchmarking
d. BMC Software, Inc.

16. In financial accounting, a _________ or Statement of cash flows is a financial statement that shows a company's flow of cash. The money coming into the business is called cash inflow, and money going out from the business is called cash outflow. The statement shows how changes in balance sheet and income accounts affect cash and cash equivalents, and breaks the analysis down to operating, investing, and financing activities.

a. BMC Software, Inc.
b. 3M Company
c. Cash flow statement
d. BNSF Railway

17. A _________ is the transfer of wealth from one party (such as a person or company) to another. A _________ is usually made in exchange for the provision of goods, services or both, or to fulfill a legal obligation.

The simplest and oldest form of _________ is barter, the exchange of one good or service for another.

a. Payee
b. Payment
c. 3M Company
d. BMC Software, Inc.

18. The _________ is a financial ratio that measures whether or not a firm has enough resources to pay its debts over the next 12 months. It compares a firm's current assets to its current liabilities. It is expressed as follows:

$$\text{Current ratio} = \frac{\text{Current Assets}}{\text{Current Liabilities}}$$

For example, if WXY Company's current assets are $50,000,000 and its current liabilities are $40,000,000, then its _________ would be $50,000,000 divided by $40,000,000, which equals 1.25.

a. Net Interest Income
b. Times interest earned
c. Current ratio
d. Return on capital

19. _________ is a financial metric which represents operating liquidity available to a business. Along with fixed assets such as plant and equipment, _________ is considered a part of operating capital. It is calculated as current assets minus current liabilities.

a. 3M Company
b. BMC Software, Inc.
c. Working capital management
d. Working capital

20. In economics, business, retail, and accounting, a _________ is the value of money that has been used up to produce something, and hence is not available for use anymore. In economics, a _________ is an alternative that is given up as a result of a decision. In business, the _________ may be one of acquisition, in which case the amount of money expended to acquire it is counted as _________.

a. Prime cost
b. Cost of quality
c. Cost
d. Cost allocation

21. In accounting, a _________ is an asset on the balance sheet which is expected to be sold or otherwise used up in the near future, usually within one year, or one business cycle - whichever is longer. Typical _________s include cash, cash equivalents, accounts receivable, inventory, the portion of prepaid accounts which will be used within a year, and short-term investments.

On the balance sheet, assets will typically be classified into _________s and long-term assets.

a. Pro forma
b. General ledger
c. Deferred
d. Current asset

22. In accounting, _________ are considered liabilities of the business that are to be settled in cash within the fiscal year or the operating cycle, whichever period is longer.

For example accounts payable for goods, services or supplies that were purchased for use in the operation of the business and payable within a normal period of time would be _________.

Bonds, mortgages and loans that are payable over a term exceeding one year would be fixed liabilities.

a. Payroll
b. Closing entries
c. Treasury stock
d. Current liabilities

23. In economics, the concept of the _________ refers to the decision-making time frame of a firm in which at least one factor of production is fixed. Costs which are fixed in the _________ have no impact on a firms decisions. For example a firm can raise output by increasing the amount of labour through overtime.

a. Short-run
b. Long-run
c. 3M Company
d. BMC Software, Inc.

24. In finance, the _________ or quick ratio or liquid ratio measures the ability of a company to use its near cash or quick assets to immediately extinguish or retire its current liabilities. Quick assets include those current assets that presumably can be quickly converted to cash at close to their book values.

$$\text{Quick (Acid Test) Ratio} = \frac{\text{Cash} + \text{Marketable Securities} + \text{Accounts Receivables}}{\text{Current Liabilities}}$$

Generally, the acid test ratio should be 1:1 or better, however this varies widely by industry.

a. Inventory turnover
b. Acid-test
c. Invested capital
d. Earnings per share

25. The _________ is an equation that equals the cost of goods sold divided by the average inventory. Average inventory equals beginning inventory plus ending inventory divided by 2.

The formula for _________:

$$\text{Inventory Turnover} = \frac{\text{Cost of Goods Sold}}{\text{Average Inventory}}$$

The formula for average inventory:

$$\text{Average Inventory} = \frac{\text{Beginning inventory}+\text{Ending inventory}}{2}$$

A low turnover rate may point to overstocking, obsolescence, or deficiencies in the product line or marketing effort.

a. Earnings per share
b. Upside potential ratio
c. Inventory turnover
d. Enterprise Value/Sales

26. In financial accounting, _________ or cost of sales includes the direct costs attributable to the production of the goods sold by a company. This amount includes the materials cost used in creating the goods along with the direct labor costs used to produce the good. It excludes indirect expenses such as distribution costs and sales force costs.

a. FIFO and LIFO accounting
b. 3M Company
c. Reorder point
d. Cost of goods sold

27. _________ is one of a series of accounting transactions dealing with the billing of customers who owe money to a person, company or organization for goods and services that have been provided to the customer. In most business entities this is typically done by generating an invoice and mailing or electronically delivering it to the customer, who in turn must pay it within an established timeframe called credit or payment terms.

An example of a common payment term is Net 30, meaning payment is due in the amount of the invoice 30 days from the date of invoice.

a. Accounts Receivable
b. Accrued revenue
c. Accrual
d. Adjusting entries

28. _________ is a financial ratio that indicates the percentage of a company's assets are provided via debt. It is the ratio of total debt (the sum of current liabilities and long-term liabilities) and total assets (the sum of current assets, fixed assets, and other assets such as 'goodwill'.)

$$\text{Debt ratio} = \frac{\text{Total Debt}}{\text{Total Assets}}$$

or alternatively:

$$\text{Debt ratio} = \frac{\text{Total Liability}}{\text{Total Assets}}$$

For example, a company with $2 million in total assets and $500,000 in total liabilities would have a _________ of 25%

Like all financial ratios, a company's _________ should be compared with their industry average or other competing firms.

a. Profitability index
b. Finance lease
c. Debt ratio
d. 3M Company

29. _________ is that which is owed; usually referencing assets owed, but the term can also cover moral obligations and other interactions not requiring money. In the case of assets, _________ is a means of using future purchasing power in the present before a summation has been earned. Some companies and corporations use _________ as a part of their overall corporate finance strategy.

a. Lender
b. Debenture
c. Loan
d. Debt

30. _________ is a fee paid on borrowed assets. It is the price paid for the use of borrowed money , or, money earned by deposited funds .Assets that are sometimes lent with _________ include money, shares, consumer goods through hire purchase, major assets such as aircraft, and even entire factories in finance lease arrangements. The _________ is calculated upon the value of the assets in the same manner as upon money.

a. Insolvency
b. AIG
c. ABC Television Network
d. Interest

31. _________ relates to the cost of borrowing money. It is the price that a lender charges a borrower for the use of the lender's money. _________ is different from OPEX and CAPEX, for it relates to the capital structure of a company.

a. AIG
b. ABC Television Network
c. Interest
d. Interest expense

32. _________ is the difference between operating revenues and operating expenses, but it is also sometimes used as a synonym for EBIT and operating profit. This is true if the firm has no non-_________.

A professional investor contemplating a change to the capital structure of a firm first evaluates a firm's fundamental earnings potential (reflected by Earnings Before Interest, Taxes, Depreciation and Amortization EBITDA and EBIT), and then determines the optimal use of debt vs. equity.

a. AIG
b. AMEX
c. ABC Television Network
d. Operating income

33. A _________ is the pinnacle activity involved in selling products or services in return for money or other compensation. It is an act of completion of a commercial activity.

A _________ is completed by the seller, the owner of the goods.

a. Tertiary sector of economy
b. Sale
c. Maturity
d. High yield stock

34. In finance, _________ also known as return on investment, rate of profit or sometimes just return, is the ratio of money gained or lost on an investment relative to the amount of money invested. The amount of money gained or lost may be referred to as interest, profit/loss, gain/loss, or net income/loss. The money invested may be referred to as the asset, capital, principal, or the cost basis of the investment.

a. Capital employed
b. Debt to capital ratio
c. Theoretical ex-rights price
d. Rate of return

35. In bookkeeping, accounting, and finance, _________ are operating revenues earned by a company when it sells its products. Revenue (_________) are reported directly on the income statement as Sales or _________.

In financial ratios that use income statement sales values, 'sales' refers to _________, not gross sales.

a. Matching principle
b. Historical cost
c. Net sales
d. Deferred

36. The _________ percentage shows how profitable a company's assets are in generating revenue.

_________ can be computed as:

$$\text{ROA} = \frac{\text{Net Income - Interest Expense - Interest Tax savings}}{\text{Average Total Assets}}$$

This number tells you what the company can do with what it has, i.e. how many dollars of earnings they derive from each dollar of assets they control. Its a useful number for comparing competing companies in the same industry.

a. Return on sales
b. Statutory Liquidity Ratio
c. Return on assets
d. Capital employed

37. In business, operating margin, operating income margin, operating profit margin or _________ is the ratio of operating income (operating profit in the UK) divided by net sales, usually presented in percent.

$$\text{Operating margin} = \left(\frac{\text{Operating income}}{\text{Revenue}}\right)$$

(Relevant figures in italics)

$$\text{Operating margin} = \left(\frac{6,318}{24,088}\right) = \underline{\underline{26.23\%}}$$

It is a measurement of what proportion of a company's revenue is left over, before taxes and other indirect costs (such as rent, bonus, interest, etc.), after paying for variable costs of production as wages, raw materials, etc. A good operating margin is needed for a company to be able to pay for its fixed costs, such as interest on debt.

a. Diluted Earnings Per Share
b. Debt service coverage ratio
c. Total revenue share
d. Return on sales

38. _________ is a specific term used in companies' financial reporting from the company-whole point of view. Because that use excludes the effects of changing ownership interest, an economic measure of _________ is necessary for financial analysis from the shareholders' point of view

_________ is defined by the Financial Accounting Standards Board, or FASB, as 'the change in equity [net assets] of a business enterprise during a period from transactions and other events and circumstances from nonowner sources. It includes all changes in equity during a period except those resulting from investments by owners and distributions to owners.'

_________ is the sum of net income and other items that must bypass the income statement because they have not been realized, including items like an unrealized holding gain or loss from available for sale securities and foreign currency translation gains or losses.

a. 3M Company
b. BMC Software, Inc.
c. BNSF Railway
d. Comprehensive income

39. _________ are the earnings returned on the initial investment amount.

In the US, the Financial Accounting Standards Board (FASB) requires companies' income statements to report _________ for each of the major categories of the income statement: continuing operations, discontinued operations, extraordinary items, and net income.

The _________ formula does not include preferred dividends for categories outside of continued operations and net income.

a. Average accounting return
b. Earnings per share
c. Invested capital
d. Earnings yield

40. In accounting, _________ or carrying value is the value of an asset according to its balance sheet account balance. For assets, the value is based on the original cost of the asset less any depreciation, amortization or impairment costs made against the asset. Traditionally, a company's _________ is its total assets minus intangible assets and liabilities.

a. Book value
b. Depreciation
c. Generally accepted accounting principles
d. Matching principle

41. _________ is a form of corporation equity ownership represented in the securities. It is a stock whose dividends are based on market fluctuations. It is dangerous in comparison to preferred shares and some other investment options, in that in the event of bankruptcy, _________ investors receive their funds after preferred stock holders, bondholders, creditors, etc. On the other hand, common shares on average perform better than preferred shares or bonds over time.

a. 3M Company
b. Growth investing
c. Stock split
d. Common stock

42. _________ are payments made by a corporation to its shareholder members. It is the portion of corporate profits paid out to stockholders. When a corporation earns a profit or surplus, that money can be put to two uses: it can either be re-invested in the business (called retained earnings), or it can be paid to the shareholders as a dividend.

a. Dividend payout ratio
b. Dividend yield
c. Dividends
d. Dividend stripping

43. _________ measures the rate of return on the ownership interest (shareholders' equity) of the common stock owners. It measures a firm's efficiency at generating profits from every dollar of shareholders' equity (also known as net assets or assets minus liabilities.) It shows how well a company uses investment dollars to generate earnings growth.

a. Like for like
b. Return on capital employed
c. Return on equity
d. Sortino ratio

44. The _________ on a company stock is the company's annual dividend payments divided by its market cap, or the dividend per share divided by the price per share. It is often expressed as a percentage.

Dividend payments on preferred shares are stipulated by the prospectus.

a. Dividends
b. Dividend yield
c. Dividend stripping
d. Dividend payout ratio

45. _________ is typically a 'higher ranking' stock than voting shares, and its terms are negotiated between the corporation and the investor.

_________ usually carries no voting rights, but may carry superior priority over common stock in the payment of dividends and upon liquidation. _________ may carry a dividend that is paid out prior to any dividends being paid to common stock holders.

a. Gross income
b. Cash flow
c. Restricted stock
d. Preferred stock

46. A _________ is any one of a variety of different systems, institutions, procedures, social relations and infrastructures whereby persons trade, and goods and services are exchanged, forming part of the economy. It is an arrangement that allows buyers and sellers to exchange things. _________s vary in size, range, geographic scale, location, types and variety of human communities, as well as the types of goods and services traded.

a. Market Failure
b. Perfect competition
c. Recession
d. Market

47. _________ is an economic concept with commonplace familiarity. It is the price that a good or service is offered at, or will fetch, in the marketplace. It is of interest mainly in the study of microeconomics.

a. Spot rate
b. Transfer agent
c. Financial instruments
d. Market price

48. _________ is the price at which an asset would trade in a competitive Walrasian auction setting. _________ is often used interchangeably with open _________, fair value or fair _________, although these terms have distinct definitions in different standards, and may differ in some circumstances.

International Valuation Standards defines _________ as 'the estimated amount for which a property should exchange on the date of valuation between a willing buyer and a willing seller in an arme;s-length transaction after proper marketing wherein the parties had each acted knowledgeably, prudently, and without compulsion.'

_________ is a concept distinct from market price, which is e;the price at which one can transacte;, while _________ is e;the true underlying valuee; according to theoretical standards.

a. Debtor
b. Market value
c. Segregated portfolio company
d. Sinking fund

49. _________ in economics and business is the result of an exchange and from that trade we assign a numerical monetary value to a good, service or asset. If Alice trades Bob 4 apples for an orange, the _________ of an orange is 4 apples. Inversely, the _________ of an apple is 1/4 oranges.

a. Price discrimination
b. Discounts and allowances
c. Price
d. Transactional Net Margin Method

50. A mutual shareholder or _________ is an individual or company (including a corporation) that legally owns one or more shares of stock in a joint stock company. A company's shareholders collectively own that company. Thus, the typical goal of such companies is to enhance shareholder value.

a. Stockholder
b. 3M Company
c. Stock split
d. Growth investing

51. In finance, the term _________ describes the amount in cash that returns to the owners of a security. Normally it does not include the price variations, at the difference of the total return. _________ applies to various stated rates of return on stocks (common and preferred, and convertible), fixed income instruments (bonds, notes, bills, strips, zero coupon), and some other investment type insurance products (e.g. annuities.)

a. Disclosure
b. Pension System
c. Residence trusts
d. Yield

52. The _________ is an expected return that the provider of capital plans to earn on their investment.

Capital (money) used for funding a business should earn returns for the capital providers who risk their capital. For an investment to be worthwhile, the expected return on capital must be greater than the _________.

a. BMC Software, Inc.
b. Capital flight
c. 3M Company
d. Cost of capital

53. In corporate finance, _________ or _________ is an estimate of true economic profit after making corrective adjustments to GAAP accounting, including deducting the opportunity cost of equity capital. _________ can be measured as Net Operating Profit After Taxes(or NOPAT) less the money cost of capital. _________ is similar in nature to that of calculating another financial performance measure - Residual Income , however, there are a few complexities involved with coming up with the elements for calculating _________ over RI such as the myriad adjustments that might be made to NOPAT before it is suitable for the formula below.

a. Internal control
b. International Monetary Fund
c. Outsourcing
d. Economic value added

54. A loan is a type of debt. Like all debt instruments, a loan entails the redistribution of financial assets over time, between the _________ and the borrower.

In a loan, the borrower initially receives or borrows an amount of money, called the principal, from the _________, and is obligated to pay back or repay an equal amount of money to the _________ at a later time.

a. Loan to value
b. Debt
c. Credit rating
d. Lender

55. _________ refers to the additional value of a commodity over the cost of commodities used to produce it from the previous stage of production. An example is the price of gasoline at the pump over the price of the oil in it. In national accounts used in macroeconomics, it refers to the contribution of the factors of production, i.e., land, labor, and capital goods, to raising the value of a product and corresponds to the incomes received by the owners of these factors.

a. Minimum wage
b. Value added
c. 3M Company
d. Supply-side economics

56. A _________ is a type of debt Like all debt instruments, a _________ entails the redistribution of financial assets over time, between the lender and the borrower.

a. Loan to value
b. Lender
c. Loan
d. Debenture

57. In economic models, the _________ time frame assumes no fixed factors of production. Firms can enter or leave the marketplace, and the cost (and availability) of land, labor, raw materials, and capital goods can be assumed to vary. In contrast, in the short-run time frame, certain factors are assumed to be fixed, because there is not sufficient time for them to change.

a. 3M Company
b. Short-run
c. BMC Software, Inc.
d. Long-run

58. A _________, also referred to as a note payable in accounting, is a contract where one party (the maker or issuer) makes an unconditional promise in writing to pay a sum of money to the other (the payee), either at a fixed or determinable future time or on demand of the payee, under specific terms. They differ from IOUs in that they contain a specific promise to pay, rather than simply acknowledging that a debt exists.

The terms of a note typically include the principal amount, the interest rate if any, and the maturity date.

a. Promissory note
b. 3M Company
c. BMC Software, Inc.
d. BNSF Railway

59. In physics, and more specifically kinematics, _________ is the change in velocity over time. Because velocity is a vector, it can change in two ways: a change in magnitude and/or a change in direction. In one dimension, _________ is the rate at which something speeds up or slows down.

a. AIG
b. ABC Television Network
c. Acceleration
d. AMEX

60. _________ refers to any one of several methods by which a company, for 'financial accounting' and/or tax purposes, depreciates a fixed asset in such a way that the amount of depreciation taken each year is higher during the earlier years of an assete;s life. For financial accounting purposes, _________ is generally used when an asset is expected to be much more productive during its early years, so that depreciation expense will more accurately represent how much of an assete;s usefulness is being used up each year. For tax purposes, _________ provides a way of deferring corporate income taxes by reducing taxable income in current years, in exchange for increased taxable income in future years.

a. Effective marginal tax rates
b. User charge
c. Indirect tax
d. Accelerated depreciation

61. _________ is a term used in accounting, economics and finance to spread the cost of an asset over the span of several years.

In simple words we can say that _________ is the reduction in the value of an asset due to usage, passage of time, wear and tear, technological outdating or obsolescence, depletion, inadequacy, rot, rust, decay or other such factors.

In accounting, _________ is a term used to describe any method of attributing the historical or purchase cost of an asset across its useful life, roughly corresponding to normal wear and tear.

a. Net profit
b. General ledger
c. Depreciation
d. Current asset

62. _________ represents claims for which formal instruments of credit are issued as evidence of debt, such as a promissory note. The credit instrument normally requires the debtor to pay interest and extends for time periods of 60-90 days or longer.

a. Public offering
b. Notes receivable
c. Restricted stock
d. Moving average

63. A _________, also client, buyer or purchaser is the buyer or user of the paid products of an individual or organization, mostly called the supplier or seller. This is typically through purchasing or renting goods or services.

a. BNSF Railway
b. 3M Company
c. BMC Software, Inc.
d. Customer

Chapter 1

1. c	2. d	3. d	4. d	5. a	6. d	7. d	8. c	9. a	10. d
11. d	12. d	13. a	14. d	15. d	16. d	17. a	18. c	19. d	20. b
21. a	22. d	23. d	24. d	25. b	26. d	27. d	28. a	29. d	30. d
31. a	32. a	33. c	34. d	35. b	36. a	37. b	38. a	39. d	40. d
41. c	42. d	43. c	44. d	45. a	46. b	47. c	48. d	49. b	50. c
51. c	52. d	53. c	54. a	55. b	56. b	57. c	58. c	59. d	60. c
61. b	62. d	63. b	64. b	65. d	66. d	67. c	68. d	69. c	70. a
71. d	72. c	73. d	74. d	75. d	76. a	77. a	78. d	79. d	80. d
81. c	82. c	83. d	84. b	85. a	86. d	87. a			

Chapter 2

1. c	2. b	3. d	4. a	5. d	6. a	7. c	8. d	9. d	10. d
11. d	12. b	13. d	14. b	15. d	16. b	17. d	18. b	19. d	20. b
21. d	22. d	23. b	24. d	25. c	26. b	27. d	28. d	29. d	30. d
31. d	32. c	33. c	34. a	35. a	36. b	37. d	38. a	39. c	40. a
41. b	42. d	43. b	44. b	45. c	46. c				

Chapter 3

1. d	2. d	3. d	4. d	5. d	6. d	7. d	8. a	9. d	10. d
11. a	12. d	13. c	14. d	15. b	16. d	17. b	18. d	19. c	20. d
21. b	22. d	23. d	24. c	25. b	26. b	27. c	28. d	29. d	30. d
31. c	32. c	33. d	34. c	35. b	36. a	37. b	38. c	39. a	40. d
41. c	42. a	43. c	44. d	45. d	46. d	47. d	48. d	49. d	50. c
51. d	52. d	53. c	54. a						

Chapter 4

1. a	2. d	3. a	4. d	5. d	6. b	7. a	8. b	9. c	10. a
11. a	12. d	13. c	14. a	15. d	16. d	17. a	18. a	19. c	20. c
21. a	22. a	23. b	24. d	25. d	26. a	27. c	28. d	29. d	30. c
31. c	32. d	33. d	34. d	35. b	36. c	37. b	38. b	39. b	40. a
41. c	42. a	43. d	44. a	45. c	46. b	47. d	48. b	49. a	50. d
51. d	52. d	53. a	54. b						

Chapter 5

1. a	2. c	3. d	4. c	5. a	6. d	7. d	8. d	9. d	10. a
11. d	12. d	13. d	14. b	15. b	16. c	17. b	18. d	19. a	20. d
21. d	22. d	23. d	24. d	25. b	26. d	27. d	28. d	29. a	30. a
31. d	32. b	33. a	34. c	35. d	36. a	37. b	38. d	39. d	40. b
41. d	42. d	43. d	44. d	45. b	46. a	47. c	48. d	49. b	50. d
51. d	52. a	53. a	54. a						

Chapter 6

1. c	2. b	3. a	4. b	5. a	6. d	7. c	8. b	9. d	10. c
11. d	12. b	13. d	14. a	15. d	16. d	17. c	18. d	19. a	20. d
21. d	22. d	23. b	24. d	25. c	26. d	27. a	28. c	29. c	30. b
31. d	32. d	33. a	34. c	35. b	36. c	37. d			

Chapter 7

1. a	2. d	3. a	4. b	5. a	6. d	7. d	8. d	9. d	10. d
11. a	12. d	13. a	14. b	15. c	16. a	17. d	18. b	19. a	20. d
21. c	22. b	23. a	24. a	25. c	26. b	27. d	28. b	29. d	30. d
31. d	32. d	33. d	34. b	35. d	36. d	37. a	38. d	39. b	40. d

Chapter 8

1. b	2. d	3. c	4. d	5. d	6. d	7. d	8. d	9. d	10. d
11. a	12. a	13. d	14. d	15. c	16. d	17. d	18. a	19. d	20. d
21. b	22. d	23. d	24. c	25. b	26. c	27. d	28. d	29. d	30. d
31. a	32. d	33. c	34. d	35. b	36. d	37. d	38. b	39. a	40. c
41. c	42. d	43. d	44. c	45. c	46. c	47. d	48. a	49. b	50. d
51. d	52. d	53. c	54. d	55. a	56. d	57. c	58. d	59. d	60. d
61. b	62. c	63. d	64. d	65. b	66. b	67. d	68. d	69. c	70. d
71. d	72. b	73. d	74. a	75. d	76. b	77. d	78. d		

Chapter 9

1. d	2. d	3. d	4. c	5. d	6. d	7. b	8. d	9. a	10. a
11. d	12. c	13. b	14. a	15. d	16. b	17. a	18. d	19. a	20. d
21. c	22. d	23. d	24. d	25. a	26. a	27. d	28. d	29. c	30. a
31. d	32. d	33. b	34. d	35. a	36. b	37. c	38. a	39. d	40. d
41. d	42. d	43. b	44. d	45. c	46. d	47. a	48. d	49. d	50. d
51. a	52. c	53. c	54. d	55. c	56. b				

Chapter 10

1. c	2. d	3. d	4. d	5. d	6. b	7. d	8. b	9. d	10. d
11. d	12. b	13. c	14. d	15. b	16. c	17. d	18. a	19. d	20. d
21. b	22. d	23. d	24. b	25. d	26. d	27. b	28. b	29. c	30. a
31. d	32. d	33. d	34. d	35. c	36. c	37. b	38. b	39. b	40. a
41. d	42. b	43. d	44. c	45. d	46. b	47. d			

Chapter 11

1. a	2. d	3. c	4. a	5. d	6. d	7. d	8. d	9. d	10. a
11. d	12. a	13. d	14. d	15. d	16. d	17. c	18. c	19. c	20. a
21. a	22. d	23. d	24. d	25. d	26. d	27. c	28. b	29. b	30. b
31. b	32. a	33. d	34. b	35. a	36. c	37. c	38. b	39. d	40. a

Chapter 12

1. b	2. a	3. b	4. d	5. d	6. d	7. c	8. a	9. a	10. a
11. c	12. b	13. d	14. d	15. d	16. a	17. b	18. d	19. a	20. d
21. d	22. c	23. d	24. c	25. d	26. c	27. d	28. d	29. b	30. d
31. c	32. c	33. d	34. d	35. d	36. d	37. d	38. b	39. d	40. d
41. d	42. d	43. d	44. c	45. a					

Chapter 13

1. a	2. b	3. d	4. d	5. d	6. d	7. d	8. d	9. a	10. a
11. d	12. d	13. b	14. b	15. c	16. c	17. b	18. c	19. d	20. c
21. d	22. d	23. a	24. b	25. c	26. d	27. a	28. c	29. d	30. d
31. d	32. d	33. b	34. d	35. c	36. c	37. d	38. d	39. b	40. a
41. d	42. c	43. c	44. b	45. d	46. d	47. d	48. b	49. c	50. a
51. d	52. d	53. d	54. d	55. b	56. c	57. d	58. a	59. c	60. d
61. c	62. b	63. d							

www.ingramcontent.com/pod-product-compliance
Lightning Source LLC
Chambersburg PA
CBHW082040230426
43670CB00016B/2727
* 9 7 8 1 4 2 8 8 7 3 1 6 2 *